A CURRICULUM
FOR THE
MENTALLY RETARDED
YOUNG ADULT

Fourth Printing

A CURRICULUM

FOR THE

MENTALLY RETARDED

YOUNG ADULT

By

WILLIAM F. SNIFF

CHARLES C THOMAS • PUBLISHER
Springfield • Illinois • U.S.A.

Published and Distributed Throughout the World by
CHARLES C THOMAS • PUBLISHER
Bannerstone House
301-327 East Lawrence Avenue, Springfield, Illinois, U.S.A.

© *1962, by* CHARLES C THOMAS • PUBLISHER

ISBN 0-398-01804-9

Library of Congress Catalog Card Number: 62-18901

First Printing, 1962
Second Printing, 1967
Third Printing, 1970
Fourth Printing, 1973

*With THOMAS BOOKS careful attention is given to all details of
manufacturing and design. It is the Publisher's desire to present books that are
satisfactory as to their physical qualities and artistic possibilities and
appropriate for their particular use. THOMAS BOOKS will be true to those
laws of quality that assure a good name and good will.*

Printed in the United States of America
R-1

PREFACE

IN RECENT YEARS the educational systems in our nation have been rapidly expanding their programs to meet the needs of mentally retarded young adults. The educational programs of both the public school system and the residential schools or institutions must continue to expand and increase to adequately meet the needs of the students included in these programs.

Thus far, emphasis on education for the educable mentally retarded has been placed to a greater extent on programs at the elementary school level than at the secondary school level. However, in very recent years more and more attention has been given to developing special education programs to adequately meet the needs of mentally retarded young adults at the secondary or high school level.

The type of program needed at the secondary level is one that will broaden the experiences of the mentally retarded students and develop attitudes and personality traits which will facilitate the students' successful adjustment to life in the family, community, and job placement so that they can become self-supporting, productive members of our society.

Each community or institution that is beginning or establishing a special education program for the mentally retarded at the secondary school level must be careful to develop the most practical program possible for the particular individual community in which it is being developed. In developing the program, the school must first meet the students' needs in his own community, and then broaden the students' experiences as much as possible so that the students can meet their needs in the environment outside their own community.

For most communities and institutions, establishing such a program at the secondary level is a difficult task, because it is a relatively new experience for them. Some of the problems encountered by these communities and institutions are as follows: 1. What should be included in such a program? A curriculum or plan of study must be developed. 2. Where can we find qualified personnel to develop the curriculum and teach such a program? If a good curriculum, which includes the practical education needed in an educational program of this type, is to be developed; it should be done by qualified personnel who have had experience teaching in such programs. This experience helps acquaint them with the needs, problems, materials, etc., that are encountered in establishing the program. 3. What problems regarding transportation will arise? Expenses and facilities must be well planned. Transportation must be provided for the many field trips and work opportunities that should be a part of special education programs for the educable mentally retarded. 4. Who should be included in the special classes? How do we screen students to enroll them in and exclude them from the classes? What ages should be included in the secondary program? etc. 5. How do we evaluate such a program? There are many more problems that will arise when a community or institution attempts to plan and organize its own secondary special class program.

The author has written this book explaining the type of program that is necessary if mentally retarded young adults at the secondary school level are to receive the practical type of education that should be available to them in the school systems of most communities. This book was written by a teacher who has taught mentally retarded young adults at the secondary school level in both public school systems and institutional classes in an institution for the mentally retarded. The book includes a practical curriculum that can be used in a special class program for the educable mentally retarded young adult in both the secondary public school system and institutions for the mentally retarded.

The introduction, objectives, and curriculum that follow will provide the reader with information regarding the type of life experiences, skills, and attitudes necessary to prepare mentally retarded young adults to adjust successfully to some life situations they will encounter. The section on requirements for enrollments will obtain information regarding some of the regulations and requirements that should be considered in enrolling the students in the program.

The curriculum for this program is written in unit form. It is not necessary to teach the units in the order in which they are presented. They can be inter-changed to meet the immediate needs of the specific program in which they are taught. Time and place and other individual factors will help determine how and when the units will be taught.

At the end of this curriculum the reader will find a list of all of the film titles listed in this book along with the name of the company or source through which it can be obtained. All of these films are free materials; and in most cases, the only expenses are the postage and sometimes insurance fees for shipment. The titles are listed in alphabetical order. Following the list of film titles is an alphabetical arrangement of the companies or available sources and their addresses. This should aid the reader in ordering some of the suggested materials to be used in the teaching of the curriculum included in this book.

It is the sincere hope of the author that this curriculum will aid communities, school systems, institutions, and teachers in organizing, establishing, and teaching their special class program.

WILLIAM F. SNIFF

CONTENTS

ix

A CURRICULUM
FOR THE
MENTALLY RETARDED
YOUNG ADULT

1

INTRODUCTION

THIS CURRICULUM is an accumulation of units that have been taught by the writer who is the teacher of a special class program for the education of the mentally retarded young adult at the secondary school level. Each unit has been taught, and has been effective in helping several dischargees of an institution for the mentally retarded attain success in some of the placements that have been made in job situations and in the community. Some of these placements probably would have been successful if the student had not been enrolled in this program. However, there are many students who can attribute much of their success in adjustment to many of the habits, skills, personality traits, and attitudes that were developed and improved through participation in this program. Even many of those who would have been successful if they had not been enrolled in the program, can attribute much of their success and ease in adjustment to the fact that they were helped by the program.

Generally speaking, people learn best through concrete experiences. Therefore, any opportunity for the teacher of the mentally retarded to change an abstract idea into a concrete experience should be taken. Discussions are by nature abstract, and much of the learning situation will be lost if they are not followed by varied concrete experiences and materials which will reinforce the learning situation. It is for this reason that the field trips and practical types of experiences have been the most valuable parts of this program. The opportunity for the students to observe first hand the subjects about which they study is reinforcement for learning which is necessary for education, especially for the institutionalized person.

Many actual experiences should be provided through field trips to various places where the students might be able to work, giving them an opportunity to observe people doing the kind of work they will be doing. They also have an opportunity to talk to personnel managers and hear from them much of the same information about habits and attitudes, appearance, personality, etc., that they have heard from the teacher. This makes a much deeper impression than can be accomplished in the classroom on a unit pertaining to getting a job, and transforms classroom discussions into a real life experience.

Field trips to use public transportation; become acquainted with operations at the fire and police departments, the courts, insurance companies, social security office, employment bureaus, post office, banks, stores and businesses in the community, along with many others, can provide many opportunities to transform abstract ideas into concrete practical experiences which enhance the learning process. These concrete experiences are the learning situations that will remain in the memories of the student which will make it possible for him to recall information about the subject taught when it becomes necessary for him to use it in the future.

Real application blanks, money, checks, bank statements, bank books, loan papers, pay check statements, social security applications, income tax papers, W2 forms, birth certificates, bills, insurance policies, safety signs, restaurant menus, pay telephones, house telephones (tele-trainer sets), telephone books, classroom stores, and all available materials that can be obtained from the businesses and services in the community are used in the teaching of this curriculum. These are aids in transferring abstractions to concrete life experiences for the mentally retarded.

The teacher of this curriculum has the students of the class help him pay bills, write checks, and balance checking accounts with bank statements at the end of each month. The students help the teacher fill out his income tax papers each year. The primary purpose of this is not to teach the students all the details of filling out income tax papers for themselves, but to inform the students that they must pay income taxes, who must pay, where to pay, when to pay, how to pay, for what is this money used, is this obligation justified, do they receive any of the services from it, why and when is it taken out of their pay checks, where do they get the papers, who can help them, how important is it for them not to make a mistake, and various other factors of which the individual must be aware to be able to pay income taxes properly.

Movies and film strips are very good visual aid materials to use in an educational program of this type. Movies provide an opportunity to bring the outside world to the students. They provide a vicarious experience which, in many cases, is the next best to actually being on the scene or going to see the subject first hand. There are many excellent movies on most of the subjects listed in this curriculum. At the end of each unit there is a list of movies that can be shown to supplement the suggested activities in the classroom. These movies have been used very successfully in the special class program, and have provided the students with much information that would have taken months to teach without the help of this visual aid program. When using these movies for mentally retarded classes, the teacher must make them successful by providing much discussion and other illustrative materials to supplement the movies and help the students obtain the information the teacher wants them to learn.

All of these experiences and materials have been very important factors in the success of meeting the objectives for this special class program. These practical experiences and concrete materials are a necessity if an educational program of this type is going to meet the needs of the mentally retarded child if he is to adjust successfully to his job and in the community.

The total school program for the educable mentally retarded student should be aimed toward work placement and successful adjustment to his immediate environment. The educational program of the school for educable mentally retarded should be functional, and directed toward the future successful work placement and successful adjustment in the community.

Rehabilitation centers, vocational services, the community, and the school must work together and cooperate in the objective that each has in the problem of what to do with the mentally retarded. The objective and terminal point of all concerned in rehabilitation is to have the mentally retarded individual successfully absorbed into the community.

We should establish firmly what we are working for in the total school program for mentally retarded and carry through with it. We do not train pupils for specific jobs, but general habits, attitudes, and skills that will assist the pupil in any job. The most important factor contributing to the success of the individual mentally retarded is his ability to get along with co-workers.

The two biggest problems with which mentally retarded have

trouble is not the work itself, but entering or getting the job and co-worker relationships. Therefore, how to get a job is one of the important things in training. Our job is to teach the pupil to take his own approach, develop independence, and not to have him completely dependent upon others for acquiring a job.

Selection of a job begins in the school system. It is here that he should learn the fundamentals such as work vocabulary, job applications, work habits and attitudes, budgeting of money, co-worker relationships, job benefits, what to do on vacation, etc.

What can we do to broaden our programs for this age group of the educable mentally retarded? It has been found that youngsters who have more life experiences are the ones who get along best. Therefore, the greater variety of life experiences that we can provide in our school, rehabilitation, and community program, the better are the chances the youngster has to achieve successful adjustment on the job and in the community.

Most work experiences prior to this age have been limited to the school program and school experiences. The school and rehabilitation program should, at ages fifteen and above, be broadened to include actual work experiences co-existing with the school program. There should be an actual work program for the pupils to get the experiences of the job situation, and spend part of the day in the work situation and part of the day in school learning more of the fundamentals while they are meaningful and can be put into practice. At this time, the pupil can receive the guidance he needs at the time he needs it. This type of program provides a gradual transition from school experiences to work experiences.

At a recent institute for the mentally retarded in which the writer participated, it was pointed out that one way to achieve this type of program is to begin by setting up a sort of sheltered workshop in the school. In the beginning, small craft programs will suffice. As the program develops and becomes more successful there should be a gradual transition from small crafts to a production type program using industry as a source for providing the work.

In this case, money (paying pupils wages) can be used as motivation. Even though the wages might be a few cents an hour, this is an incentive which is appealing to almost all people—retarded or not.

If this is to be successful, it must be understood that this program is not intended to support itself, just as we do not expect other educational programs to support themselves.

It was understood that this is a somewhat idealistic undertaking, but if we are ever to broaden our programs to include the life experiences that are the most meaningful and practical to accomplish the aims we have in the education and rehabilitation of the mentally retarded, we must plan and work toward this goal.

How can referrals be made from a school program to other community programs? One method of referral from school to other community programs is of course through school teachers and administration directly. In this case, teachers and school administrators must make the contacts for job placements or other community programs.

Another method of referral that has been used is the parents. Mothers and fathers (parents groups) are often used as the media between school and a program to follow. They often raise money and develop interest in the community to develop further programs and placement. It is not intended for them to promote interest of their own child only, but a program for the total community.

Another suggested source of referral from school to a program to follow in the community are the civic clubs and social organizations of the community to which the business men and leaders of the community belong such as the Rotary Clubs, Kiwanis Clubs, Lions Clubs, Chamber of Commerce and others of this type. This is an excellent source because the members of these clubs are often the very people who are the employers with potential for hiring the mentally retarded.

Rehabilitation and education should incorporate with it evaluation to determine who should be selected from the school program. There must be evaluation to set up the correct program for the educable—be it work placement or other. Evaluation and research must be done to determine the success of the program. All job placements must be investigated to find out which jobs tend to be the most successful and what factors contribute to this success on these particular jobs. The evaluation that has been done can be used as an aid to improve and further develop the education and rehabilitation program. The education and rehabilitation program itself can be a source of referral to its own program.

As mentioned before, the terminal goal of the vocational rehabilitation program is job placement. At a recent institute attended by the writer, a discussion arose regarding the policy of not labeling the mentally retarded as mentally retarded when referring them to people in the community for job placement. In the debate that followed it was pointed out that the process of calling mentally retardeds slow learners, shy, limited, etc., is not necessarily misrepresentation, nor is the process of selling the abilities and not the disabilities of the mentally retarded misrepresentation. In fact this usually is the only advisable and sensible way of approaching the community business people when making a successful placement. Referring to the special class student as mentally retarded tends to set up a mental or emotional block, which prevents many people in the community from participating in an active program for the mentally retarded.

I would like to close this discussion regarding the type of program necessary for rehabilitation and education of the educable mentally retarded with a quotation from the booklet entitled *Wisconsin Public School Services for Retarded Children;* by Kenneth R. Blessing, Daniel Mathias, and Floyd L. Baribeau, Supervisors of Classes for Exceptional Children, Madison, Wisconsin, 1958, pp. 62 & 63.

"The Need for Within-School and Community Work Experience Programs for the Mentally Retarded.

"For youth of secondary school age, work experience programs are very beneficial in keeping the students in school, vocational guidance is of utmost importance, because high school provides terminal education for these youths. In some of the schools, practical work experiences of a pre-vocational nature are arranged for selected retarded youth. Work in cafeterias, supply rooms, and as attendance clerks are examples of duties they can perform. In order to insure smooth running of this type of within school program, it is necessary to: 1. Survey jobs available, primarily for educational purpose rather than for busy work; 2. Assign a capable advisor so as to incorporate work into curriculum; 3. Provide time for counselor or special teacher to supervise work after satisfactory placement is made; 4. Evaluate performance and give credit for work performed; 5. Counsel student on proper work habits, attitudes; and 6. Aid in student adjustment to the working world.

"A community experience program is often the adhesive that keeps the slow learner in school. It gives him a positive sample of what adult life has to offer and yet impresses him with his need for more education. It affords the special class teacher the opportunity to relate work in the academic areas to the job experiences of his special pupils.

"A secondary school special class teacher should have a schedule that allows working with cooperating employers and labor unions in the community. Thus, he can relate the content of his teaching in the classroom to the actual working conditions of his adolescent pupils. This type of programming stresses the direct needs for language and communication and gives the instructor a direct avenue for person-to-person guidance conferences.

"The work experience program of the special department is the key transitional step between the classroom and 'open' employment in the community. It should be a time for preparing the slow learner for his role as a self-sufficient citizen. The per capita cost of this work experience program is often large, but the money is truly well spent when a marginal citizen becomes an independent rather than a dependent member of our society. It is especially in this area of school work experience programs that close team work and liaison between the public school, Industrial Commission and Vocational Rehabilitation is essential."

2

OBJECTIVES

THE SPECIAL class program for the mentally retarded young adult at the secondary school level should be organized to help the individual understand himself as an individual and as a member of a group or groups so that he may make the best possible adjustment in the community in which he lives and works—be it the institutional community or any other type of community of which he might be a member.

It is the purpose of the program to provide the students with an understanding of what a community is, including what services it offers its members, how these services can be utilized, the responsibilities of the community to its members, and the responsibilities of the individual to the community in which he lives.

After an understanding of the meaning of a community and its functions is reached, the classes should begin the study of the individual himself. A community should be more successful when the individual citizens know what their roles in the life of the community and its functions are. Areas of study include personal health and hygiene, sanitation, proper diet, good posture, exercise, and fresh air; and how these factors affect one's health and personal happiness. The fact that the welfare of the community depends upon the attitudes, health and happiness of its individual members is an important consideration in helping the students understand their role in the life of the community.

In terms of preparation for adjustment to work placement and life as a citizen in the community, the age group 15 to 20 is a very crucial period of development in the lives of the mentally retarded individual. During this period he is developing personality traits, building character, forming habits and attitudes, developing vocabulary for life and work, forming work patterns, and learning skills which will shape the pattern of his life and determine his future success or failure. Our objective is to help each individual develop in all of these areas to the maximum of his ability.

The educational program facilitates adjustment to work placement. The objectives for the educational program for educable mentally retarded should be functional and directed toward future successful work placement and successful adjustment to the community. The objective is not to train pupils for specific jobs, but to produce general habits, attitudes, and skills that assist the student in any job or community placement.

Our objectives include preparing the individual to adjust successfully to his role and acquire the necessary skills and information in the following areas of living:

I. Understanding the community
   A. What is a community?
   B. Functions or responsibilities of a community to its citizens:
      1. Who is a citizen?
      2. Responsibilities of a citizen to his community
      3. Responsibilities of a community to its citizens
         —Community helpers
         —Education
         —Recreation
         —Transportation
         —Sanitation
         —Communication
         —Emergencies
         —Protection
II. Using community resources
   A. Emergencies
      1. Telephone
      2. Fire
      3. Police
      4. Doctors
      5. Natural emergencies
   B. Communication
      1. Letters
      2. Postal services
      3. Telegrams
      4. Telephone

    C. Banks and credit
       1. Budgeting
       2. Savings accounts
       3. Checking accounts
       4. Bank credit—loans
       5. Charge accounts
       6. Easy payments
       7. Loan companies
    D. Insurances
       1. Hospitalization
       2. Medical
       3. Disability
       4. Life
       5. Automobile
       6. Property
    E. Voting
    F. Legal requirements and services
       1. Social security
       2. Birth certificate
       3. Draft registration
       4. Personal identification
       5. Taxes
       6. Driving a car
    G. Social community resources
       1. Finding a place to live—type of homes
       2. Church membership
       3. Use of alcoholic beverages
III. Self care and personal development
    A. Personal appearance
       1. Cleanliness
       2. Good posture
       3. Care of all parts of the body
       4. Neat and clean clothes
    B. Balanced diets—eating right kinds of food
    C. Other factors contributing to good health
       1. Fresh air and exercise
       2. Care of illnesses and ailments
       3. Mental hygiene

D. Manners and courtesy
   1. Table manners
   2. Personal manners
   3. Group manners
   4. Conduct in public places
E. Care of personal and public property
   1. Personal property
   2. Public property

IV. Getting and keeping a job
  A. Employment services—getting the job
    1. Kinds of jobs available
    2. Qualifications necessary
    3. Employment services available
    4. Union regulations
    5. Interviews and job benefits
  B. Time for work
  C. Getting to work
  D. Transportation
  E. Use of maps
  F. Where to eat
  G. Vacation
  H. Social Security and Old Age Pensions

V. Family
  A. The family unit
  B. Parents' responsibilities
  C. Children's responsibilities
  D. Family finances:
    1. Sources of family income
    2. Family expenses
  E. The family and the community
  F. The home
    1. Choosing a place to live
    2. Furnishing a home
    3. Care of the home

VI. Making friends
  A. What is a good friend
  B. Where can you find them
  C. How can you get acquainted

VII. Money
  A. Recognition of money
  B. Realization of value of coins and bills
  C. How do we count money
  D. How do we write the values of money
  E. Budgeting money
VIII. Clothing
  A. Needs
  B. Purchases
  C. Cleaning and maintenance
  IX. Recreation and use of leisure time
  A. Recreation outside the home
  B. Recreation in or near the home
  X. Safety
  A. Safety in the home
  B. Safety in the community

The educational program should provide a variety of experiences in the above areas which will enable mentally retarded youth to develop enough self-confidence to meet and solve problems that they may eventually encounter in the environment of which they are a part. In summary the objectives of an educational program for the mentally retarded include the development of a well-adjusted personality, the opportunity for self-realization, the ability to participate more adequately in human relationships, the opportunity to function as a law-abiding citizen of the community, state, and nation, and the opportunity to become economically secure and self-supporting.

3

SOME FACTORS TO BE CONSIDERED IN PLACEMENT OF STUDENTS IN A SPECIAL EDUCATION PROGRAM FOR THE EDUCABLE MENTALLY RETARDED AT THE SECONDARY SCHOOL LEVEL

EACH STUDENT should receive personal consideration in terms of his intellectual, physical, emotional, and social adaptability to the program for the educable mentally retarded at the secondary school level. The following regulations and suggestions for placement should not be interpreted too rigidly. It is not absolutely necessary to adhere to each and every requirement, since specific individual qualities sometimes merit dispensing with certain requirements. Certain individual state and local requirements and regulations will affect the suggestions offered below for enrolling students in the programs of the various different states and local communities where the program is being established.

1. Chronological ages should range from *approximately* fifteen to twenty years. Institutional programs will include older students.

2. The student should have an intelligence quotient of *approximately* 50 or above to be considered for the educational program for the *educable* mentally retarded. The upper I.Q. limit will be determined by the proper authorities of the state in which the program is being established.

3. The student should be in such physical condition that would merit placement in the program. He should be ambulatory, have control over his toilet habits, have adequate sight and hearing to function independently, and possess speech sufficient to communicate his needs, wants, and desires.

4. The student should be free of *major* personality disorders so that he does not hinder the progress of other people in the class. He should have the potential to develop sufficient social competence to become acceptable enough to live in the community. In

15

the institutional setting he should possess sufficient emotional stability to merit consideration for discharge from the institution. 5. The student should have a felt need for his placement, and he should clearly understand that he will be excluded from the program if he does not prove himself to be mature enough to merit his continuation in the program when the law permits such action to be taken.

4

THE CURRICULUM

UNDERSTANDING THE COMMUNITY

Objectives:

1. To develop an understanding of what a community is
2. To learn the responsibilities of a community to its citizens
3. To learn the responsibilities of a citizen to his community
4. To learn how to use the services available for us in the community

Content Outline:

I. Understanding the community:
   A. Definition of a community:
      A community is a group or groups of people living and working together within a geographical area.
   B. Functions or responsibilities of a community to its citizens
      1. Education:
         a. School
         b. Church
         c. Library
         d. Museum
         e. Radio
         f. Television
         g. Clubs—4-H, etc.
      2. Recreation
         a. Clubs or social organizations
            (1) 4-H Club
            (2) Scouts—boy and girl
         b. Church
         c. School
         d. Y.M.C.A.—Y.W.C.A.
         e. Parks and zoos
         f. Play grounds
         g. Golf courses
         h. Theaters
         i. Dance halls
         j. Roller skating rinks
         k. Ice skating
         l. Swimming pools
         m. Bowling alleys
         n. Dining places

UNDERSTANDING THE COMMUNITY

Suggested Activities:

I. Understanding the community:
   1. Discussions about the community to help pupils understand what the community is and the responsibilities it has to its citizens.
   2. Discussions about citizens: Who are citizens—what makes us a citizen —what are our responsibilities as a citizen, etc.
   3. Discussions about where we live: What country—what state—what county—what city—what community?
   4. Study maps showing these places.
   5. Take walks around our own community pointing out how our community is meeting the responsibilities discussed in class. Point out how the community is meeting the needs of its citizens.
   6. Make scrap books and have the pupils find pictures of the services provided in the community. Have pupil divide his scrap book in sections showing the various types of services in separate sections such as educational services, recreational services, transportation services, etc.
   7. Have pupils make bulletin boards showing the services found in the community.
   8. Have a vocabulary study of key words in the unit such as: education —recreation—transportation—communication—emergency—services— protection—responsibilities—citizens, etc.
   9. Make a cross-word puzzle using vocabulary of words used in the unit.
   10. Suggested field trips:
      A. *Field trips around the community or institution* to show the various departments and services. This is to help the student understand the community, and illustrate how all departments and services must work together to operate successfully.
      B. *Field trips to the nearest community outside the institution* to show the students a non-institutional community in operation, if they live in an institutional setting. This is to help develop an understanding of what a community is by showing the business, industrial and residential areas of the town. The students observe some of the different kinds of stores, the post office, bank, barber shops, doctors'

UNDERSTANDING THE COMMUNITY

Content Outline:

I. Understanding the community:
  B. Functions or responsibilities of a community to its citizens:
    3. Transportation:
      a. Cars and taxi cabs
      b. Trains
        (1) subway
        (2) elevated
      c. Buses
      d. Street cars
      e. Trolley cars
    4. Sanitation
      a. Garbage collectors
      b. Junk dealers or collectors
      c. Street sweepers
      d. Inspectors
      e. Weed commissioners
      f. Zoning laws
      g. Food and drug laws
      h. Health department
    5. Communication:
      a. Telephone
      b. Telegraph
      c. Post office—mail, etc.
      d. Newspapers
      e. Radio
      f. Television

UNDERSTANDING THE COMMUNITY

Suggested Activities:

I. Understanding the community:
   B. (continued)
      offices, gas stations, laundries, cleaners, etc., to get an idea what
      one finds in a business district. They tour the residential section to
      see what is included in that area of the town. The class tours the
      whole town to give them a concept of what is needed to make a
      community, if it is to fulfill the responsibilities that have previously
      been discussed in class.
   C. *Trip to fire department*
      Students visit a fire department to learn of its function in the event
      of a fire or other emergencies. They see the equipment used, learn
      how to turn in an alarm, and learn of methods employed in times of
      crisis including life saving and safety measures. The purpose of
      this trip is to help students to know where to seek help and pro-
      tection in times of emergency.
   D. *Trip to police station*
      Students visit police station to see where they can turn for help
      and protection in an emergency.
      A policeman talks to students about the duties and responsibilities
      of the police department to the community and its citizens.
   E. *Trip to a large city to use public transportation*
      Students should learn to use public buses, street cars, elevated and
      subway trains. They should have the experiences of boarding the
      bus, paying the fair, stopping the bus at the place of departure or
      destination, etc.

UNDERSTANDING THE COMMUNITY

Content Outline:

I. Understanding the community:
  B. Functions or responsibilities of a community to its citizens:
    6. Emergencies and services (miscellaneous) :
      a. Hospitals
        (1) doctors
        (2) nurses
        (3) etc.
      b. Dentist
      c. Fire departments
      d. Police stations
      e. Courts and lawyers
      f. Telephone
      g. Plumbers
      h. Veterinarians
      i. Electricians
      j. Laundries, dry cleaners and tailors
      k. Employment bureaus
      l. Bank
      m. Local businesses of all kinds
        (1) Department stores
        (2) Grocery stores, etc.
        (3) Gas stations
      n. Moving companies
      o. Trucking companies
      p. Post offices
      q. Insurance companies
      r. Construction companies

UNDERSTANDING THE COMMUNITY

Suggested Activities:

I. Understanding the community:
    10. Suggested field trips: (Continued)
        F. Advantage should be taken of any opportunity to take field trips to any other services of the community.
    11. Show movies and film strips about the services found in the community. The following are suggested movies that can be shown with this unit of work. These movies are listed in the back of this book:
        A. *Even for One*
        B. *Another Light*
        C. *Story of Human Energy*
        D. *Medicine Man*
        E. *Rabies Control in the Community*
        F. *Friend of a Friend*
        G. *Collector's Item*
        H. *Community Vector Control*
        I. *Engineering Your Health*
        J. *Rat Killing*
        K. *The Rat Problem*
        L. *Survey of Refuse Disposal Methods*
        M. *Pure Water and Public Health*
        N. *Hospital Clean*
        O. *Man on the Lands*
        P. *50,000 Lives*
        Q. *A Morning With Jimmy*

USING COMMUNITY RESOURCES

Objectives:

1. To become familiar with possible emergency situations and to learn what what to do under such circumstances.
2. To be made aware of resources and services that are provided by the community and learn how these resources can be utilized.

Content Outline:

II. Using community resources:
   A. Emergencies:
      1. Telephone
         a. Use of the phone book
            (1) Location of emergency numbers
            (2) Yellow pages
            (3) White pages
         b. Getting the number
            (1) Operator will accept information even without the number
            (2) Dial
            (3) Be specific with directions
         c. Proper use of the telephone
            (1) Social
            (2) Business
            (3) Conversation

USING COMMUNITY RESOURCES

Suggested Activities:

II. Using community resources:
   A. Emergencies:
      1. Telephone
         a. Obtain phone books from various nearby communities for group use. Class should become familiar with how the names are listed and location of emergency numbers.
         b. Discussion on importance of always looking up the number in the book. Distinguish between home and classified sections and practice looking up numbers picked at random.
         c. Discuss value of listing numbers of friends we call often or numbers we might need to call in an emergency.
         d. Discussion of what would constitute an emergency call. Find the emergency numbers in various books. Point out that information can be given to operator without the number on a non-dial phone.
         e. Present demonstration on the proper way to dial a call and have the group practice on actual phones. Discuss the importance of remaining calm and talking slowly and distinctly.
         f. Discussion on fact that you are judged by your voice and conversation on phone call as other party cannot see you. Emphasizing politeness and necessity of hanging up immediately if given wrong number.
         g. Discuss importance of not being a "party line piggy." Release party line immediately for any emergency call. Never slam receiver down but place it carefully on hook or stand.
         h. Discuss importance of never talking with anything in your mouth. Class participants could make imaginative social calls, employing all of the above telephone courtesies.
         i. Review the use of the classified section of the telephone directory. Discussion of business people or businesses and what might constitute a business telephone call.
         j. Members of the group could suggest and make various business calls.
         k. Discuss importance of and practice proper telephone conversation.

USING COMMUNITY RESOURCES

Content Outline:

II. Using community resources:
  A. Emergencies:
    2. Fire
      a. Calling the fire department by phone.
        (1) Use emergency numbers
        (2) Give proper directions
      b. Turning in alarm at call box.
        (1) Stay there until apparatus comes
    3. Police
      a. Accidents
        (1) Personal
        (2) Auto
      b. Prowler
        (1) Has anything been stolen
        (2) Property damaged
      c. Disturbances
        (1) Fighting
        (2) Disrupting the peace
        (3) Drinking

USING COMMUNITY RESOURCES

Suggested Activities:

II. Using community resources:
   A. Emergencies:
      2. Fire
         a. Discussion that in case of fire that it is important to find and use emergency numbers in front of book.
         b. Group can compile a list of what directions to give in case of fire.
         c. Group can make imaginative fire calls, looking up emergency numbers in phone book, dialing or giving the operator the number and the correct information and directions.
         d. Discussion on turning in an alarm at an alarm box pointing out the use of box as best, if it is closer than a phone. Group can be taken to a fire alarm box for demonstration.
         e. Arrangements might be made for some practice on alarm box. Discussion of directions and proper procedure should be held.
         f. Particular emphasis in discussion on the importance of speed in turning in the alarm either by phone or at the box.
      3. Police
         a. Discussion on what the policeman can do for you. Bring out the activities of the police in accidents, protecting you and your property and preserving the peace.
         b. Have group compile a list of situations in which they could use the help of a policeman.
         c. View and discuss visual materials on the role of the policeman.
         d. Discussion on how you would find a policeman and what to tell him in an emergency situation. What about rural?
         e. Have members of the group act out the role of the policeman and the citizen.

USING COMMUNITY RESOURCES

Content Outline:

II. Using community resources:
  A. Emergencies:
    4. Doctor
      a. Accidents
        (1) Home
        (2) Street
      b. Illnesses
        (1) Office call
        (2) Home visitation
    5. Natural
      a. Drowning
        (1) Swim only with others
        (2) Not immediately after eating
      b. Storm
        (1) Lightning
        (2) High winds

USING COMMUNITY RESOURCES

Suggested activities:

II. Using community resources:
  A. Emergencies:
    4. Doctor
      a. Discussion on when to call the doctor and where to find one. Bring out the fact that there are different kinds of doctors and that specialties exist.
      b. Compare the costs of various kinds of medical service and survey availability of free care.
      c. Discussion on what to tell the doctor if you call one. Be able to describe how you feel.
    5. Natural
      a. Discussion on the dangers of drowning and the importance of never swimming alone or right after eating.
      b. Discussion on electrical storms and lightning pointing out that most electrical discharges are between clouds and that thunder is only noise.
      c. Compile list of safety directions that will apply during an electrical storm. Where would it be safe and where not so safe.
      d. Discussion on what to do in case of very high winds. Point out that it is better to enter a substantial building or lie on the ground if caught in the open.

USING COMMUNITY RESOURCES

Content Outline:

II. Using community resources:
  B. Communication:
    1. How to write a letter
      a. Mechanics of letter
      b. Correct address
    2. Postage
      a. Weight (class)
      b. Regular
      c. Special delivery
      d. Air Mail
      e. Registered mail
    3. Where to mail it
      a. Mail box (schedule for pick up)
      b. Post Office (issues money orders)
      c. Always notify of change in address
    4. Packages
      a. Size
      b. Weight
      c. Zones
      d. Cost
      e. How to wrap
      f. Correct address and return address
    5. Telegram
      a. What are they
      b. Rates (day and night)

USING COMMUNITY RESOURCES

Suggested Activities:

II. Using community resources:
  B. Communication:
    1. Class discussion on various types of letters including both friendly and business letters. What kinds of postage are there?
    2. Practice writing individual letters with each student choosing his own type.
    3. Discussion on what happens to a letter after you mail it. Send different letters to various class members noting the kind of stamp necessary, cost of the postage and the time to make delivery.
    4. Visit the post office or local mailing facility for a demonstration. Follow-up discussion for answering any questions.
    5. Discussion on how to mail a package emphasizing good wrapping and correct address and postage. Provide class practice on wrapping packages.
    6. Discussion on what a telegram is and when you would send one. Distribute blanks and compose some telegrams.
    7. View and discuss all available visual materials.

USING COMMUNITY RESOURCES

Content Outline:

II. Using community resources:
  C. Banks and credit
    1. Planning an adequate budget
    2. Savings accounts
      a. Making regular deposits in person or by mail
    3. Checking accounts
      a. Need and cost
      b. How to write checks
      c. How to balance check book with bank statement
    4. Bank credit
      a. Loans for specific purposes
      b. Security
    5. Charge accounts
      a. What are they
      b. Determine the total cost
    6. "Easy payments"
      a. What are they
      b. Determine the total cost
    7. Loan companies
      a. How do they work
      b. Cost

USING COMMUNITY RESOURCES

Suggested Activities:

II. Using community resources:
   C. Banks and credit:
      1. Discussion on what a bank is and how you would open an account. Answer question as to what happens to your money in a bank.
      2. Discussion on what kinds of accounts there are in a bank and what each kind is used for. Pass out sample deposit and withdrawal slips, bank books, bank checks, etc.
      3. Practice writing checks.
      4. Learn vocabulary on check stub.
      5. How does a bank loan money? Visit the local bank for a demonstration of its functions.
      6. Conduct banking activities in the classroom covering the various activities involved.
      7. Discuss the importance of saving money and always paying your bills (credit rating).
      8. What is a credit rating? How is it useful? Discussion on charge accounts and easy payment plans. What are their dangers.
      9. Discussion on loan companies as to how they work. Dramatize someone coming in to make a loan. What has to be considered?

USING COMMUNITY RESOURCES

Content Outline:

II. Using community resources:
  D. Insurance:
    1. Purpose of insurance:
      We carry insurance for financial (money) protection against the tragedies and inconveniences of life.
    2. Kinds of insurance:
      a. Hospitalization insurance—Ex. 1—Blue Cross
                                       Ex. 2—White Cross
        (1) Pays hospital bills
          (a) Hospital services (in part or in full)
          (b) Hospital medication
      b. Medical insurance—Ex.—Blue Shield
        (1) Pays doctor bills
        (2) Pays for certain medication
      c. Disability insurance (Health and Accident):
        (1) Pays benefits to individuals, who, because of sickness or accidents, are unable to work for a period of time or for life.
      d. Life insurance
        (1) Provides protection for beneficiaries of the insured in the event of his death—beneficiaries receive the amount of the insurance policy when the insured person dies.
        (2) Provides a kind of savings account for the insured in the event that he lives out a full life time.
          (a) The insured can sometimes borrow money on the amount he has already paid into the company.
          (b) The company often pays interest or dividends to the insured for the use of his money.
          (c) The insured can sometimes draw out the amount invested in the company after a certain period of time.
          (d) The insured can receive the full amount of the policy and its interest after it has been paid in full (either in small payments or the full amount).

USING COMMUNITY RESOURCES

Suggested Activities:

II. Using community resources:
   D. Insurance:
      1. Discussion on purpose of insurance—What is insurance?
      2. Discussions on different kinds of insurances.
      3. Vocabulary study on terms used in insurance policies such as: beneficiary—premium—annual—semi-annual—dividend—insured, etc.
      4. Bring real insurance policies of various kinds to class and go over them with students. Study important features of each kind.
      5. Discussion on insurance costs—how paid, etc. Select individuals for examples and plan an adequate insurance program for each.
      6. Have class prepare a list of questions to ask an insurance salesman when he is trying to sell them insurance. Have class prepare a list of questions for each kind of insurance and keep it in their note books.
      7. Have each pupil make a notebook including vocabulary study—various insurance policies, class work on unit such as the list of questions to ask insurance salesman, etc.
      8. Take field trip to an insurance office and have life insurance salesman demonstrate his procedure in selling insurance to his customer just as though the class members were his customers. Have him explain his policy, its benefits, etc. to them.
      9. Show movies on insurances to class. Some suggested movies are:

From Every Mountainside	Modern No. 213
Measure of a Man	Modern No. 788
Two Cheers for Charlie	Sterling Movies, Inc.
Peace of Mind	Sterling Movies, Inc.

USING COMMUNITY RESOURCES

Content Outline:

II. Using community resources:
   D. Insurance:
      2. Kinds of insurance: (continued)
         e. Automobile insurance
           (1) Personal liability and property damage
              (a) Protects insured from law suits
           (2) Collision
              (a) Pays for all—part, or certain percentage of car repair, or replaces car, or pays value of car to insured at time of accident
           (3) Comprehensive—fire, wind, theft, broken windows, etc.
           (4) Legal requirements
         f. Home insurance
           (1) Fire, wind, theft, etc.
   E. Voting:
      1. Who can vote
         a. Age
         b. Registration
      2. When and where does one vote
         a. According to residence
         b. Specified election days
      3. How is it done
         a. Marking the ballot
         b. Voting machine
      4. Candidates
         a. Stand on issues made public
         b. Use own judgment

USING COMMUNITY RESOURCES

Suggested Activities:

II. Using community resources:
   E. Voting:
      1. Discussion on the American Heritage and the importance of the right to vote in a democratic form of government.
      2. Survey the current political campaigns and try to develop the fundamental issues involved.
      3. Show how candidates for political office are chosen and how the citizen votes for them. Obtain sample ballots with candidates names on them and show how to mark the ballot.
      4. Follow candidates on press and radio and television and discuss their views in class. Conduct mock election in the class room for various national offices.

USING COMMUNITY RESOURCES

Content Outline:

II. Using community resources:
  F. Legal requirements and services
    1. Social security card
       a. Where to apply
       b. Necessary in most employment
    2. Birth certificate
       a. Register of deeds (court house)
       b. Necessary in some employment
    3. Draft registration
       a. All men must register (age limits)
    4. Personal identification
       a. Always carry on person
    5. Taxes
       a. Who must file an income tax
       b. Proper form to use
       c. Who will help
       d. Excise taxes
    6. Driving a car
       a. License
       b. Parking regulations
       c. Parking meters

USING COMMUNITY RESOURCES

Suggested Activities

II. Using community resources:
    F. Legal requirements and services
        1. Discussion on what legal restrictions are likely to affect the individual.
        2. Obtain samples of social security card, birth certificate, draft registration and personal identification.
        3. Discussion on where and how to apply for each. Provide the actual practice in the classroom.
        4. Discussion on taxes as to who must pay, when and where to file and how it is done. Use proper forms for demonstrations.
        5. Discussion on legal requirements for driving a car and what problems are likely to be encountered in driving.
        6. View visual materials and discuss rules of safety for both the motorist and the pedestrian.

USING COMMUNITY RESOURCES

Content Outline

II. Using community resources:
   G. Social
      1. Finding a place to live:
         a. Kinds of homes available
           (1) Single rooms
              (a) Y.M.C.A. or Y.W.C.A.
              (b) Rooming houses
              (c) Private homes
              (d) Hotels
           (2) Apartments
           (3) Houses
              (a) Renting a house
              (b) Owning a house
           (4) Mobile homes
         b. Methods of finding a place to live
           (1) Watch classified ads in newspapers
           (2) Telephone
           (3) Friends
           (4) Minister
         c. Things to consider in finding a place to live
           (1) Nearness to job
           (2) Cost must be suitable to individual's budget
           (3) Home furnishings required

USING COMMUNITY RESOURCES

Suggested Activities

II. Using community resources:
  G. Social
    1. Discussion on kinds of homes available.
    2. Discussion on advantages and disadvantages of all types of homes.
    3. Field trips to see various types of homes that are for rent—single room, Y.M.C.A., apartments, etc.
    4. Movies on various types of homes.
    5. Discussion on methods of finding a place to live—who can help, etc.?
    6. Class discussion on things to consider when looking for a place to live.
    7. Read and discuss the Classified Section of Newspaper—pick out one or two places to go to see if it would meet the needs required.
    8. Have pupils make notebooks including pictures of kinds of homes, home furnishings needed, classified newspaper ads, and other materials used in discussions of the unit.
    9. Use bulletin boards as visual aids in presenting materials.

USING COMMUNITY RESOURCES

Content Outline:

II. Using community resources:
    G. Social
        2. Church membership:
            a. Various denominations
            b. Reasons for belonging to a church
            c. Respect for religious denominations other than your own
            d. How to use services of a church
                (1) For worship
                (2) For recreation
                (3) For education
        3. Use of taverns and alcoholic beverages:
            a. Social drinking
            b. Expense involved
            c. Dangers of getting into trouble in many other areas because of drinking.
            d. Affects of alcoholic beverages on one's health
            e. Affects of alcoholic beverages on one's morals and attitudes
            f. The problem of alcoholics in our society

USING COMMUNITY RESOURCES

Suggested Activities:

II. Using community resources:
   G. Social:
      2. Church membership:
         a. Discussion on reasons for belonging to a Church.
         b. Discussion on having respect for religious denominations other than your own.
         c. Discussion on the services of a Church such as worship, education, and recreation.
      3. Use of taverns and alcoholic beverages:
         a. Discussions on social drinking—point out the dangers involved. Point out expenses, etc.
         b. Discussions on legal factors with which one can become involved when getting into trouble after drinking alcoholic beverages.
         c. Discussion on effects of alcoholic beverages on one's health and morals.
         d. Discussion of problems of our society that are an outgrowth of the use of alcoholic beverages.
         e. Obtain pamphlets from State Board of Health on subject of alcoholic beverages. Materials can also be obtained from State Traffic Division of Motor Vehicle Department.

USING COMMUNITY RESOURCES

Suggested Activities:

II. Using community resources:
    G. Social:
        3. Use of taverns and alcoholic beverages:
            f. Show movies and film strips on the subjects discussed in the previous suggested activities.

Theobald Faces the Facts	National W.C.T.U., Evanston, Ill.
What About Alcohol	National W.C.T.U., Evanston, Ill.
Any Boy—U.S.A.	National W.C.T.U., Evanston, Ill.
The Choice Is Yours	National W.C.T.U., Evanston, Ill.
Friendly Enemy	National W.C.T.U., Evanston, Ill.
The Brain Is the Reason	National W.C.T.U., Evanston, Ill.
Symptoms of Our Times	American Osteopathic Association Order Department, 212 East Ohio Street, Chicago 11, Illinois
The Grandview Story	National W.C.T.U., Evanston, Ill.
Fact or Fancy	National W.C.T.U., Evanston, Ill.
The Chance of a Life Time	National W.C.T.U., Evanston, Ill.
Dollars and Sense	National W.C.T.U., Evanston, Ill.

SELF CARE AND PERSONAL DEVELOPMENT

Objectives:

1. To develop regular habits of personal cleanliness, good care of the body, and social adaptability.
2. To develop proper attitudes toward health and generate good mental hygiene.
3. To develop a sense of responsibility for the proper care of clothing.
4. To develop respect for equipment and property and the rights of others.

Content Outline:

III. Self care and personal development:
   A. Personal appearance—Importance of good appearance at all times:
      1. Wash and bathe regularly (use of deodorants)
      2. Care of face
         a. Shave regularly
         b. Blackheads and pimples and how to care for them

SELF CARE AND PERSONAL DEVELOPMENT

Suggested Activities

III. Self care and personal development:
  A. Personal appearance:
    1. Wash and bathe regularly:
      a. Demonstration of proper washing of hands and face with use of soap, brush and hand cream.
      b. Showing the visual materials on the care of hands and face with discussion following.
      c. Discussion of when to wash and why with dramatizations of various situations.
      d. Discussion of bath procedures with emphasis on importance of daily shower. Use of bath as more thorough cleanser and relaxing agent.
      e. Discussion on the use of deodorants. Display of various kinds of empty deodorant containers collected by teacher including cream types, spray types, roll-on types, etc.
      f. Display of various kinds of soap wrappers, and discussion of kinds of soaps available.
    2. Care of face:
      a. Demonstrations and discussions on shaving procedures. Use of creams (brush and brushless), shaving soap and ordinary hand soap.
      b. Frequency of shaving will depend to great extent on personal needs. Better boys will be capable of using razor.
      c. Discussion of importance of good grooming and the reason for shaving.
      d. Successful passing of shaving test.
      e. Discussion on care of face. Point out causes of pimples and blackheads and how to care for them.
      f. Show movies and slide films on care of face.

SELF CARE AND PERSONAL DEVELOPMENT

Content Outline:

III. Self care and personal development:
     3. Care of nails
        a. Proper cleaning of nails
        b. Proper cutting of nails
        c. Nail biting

SELF CARE AND PERSONAL DEVELOPMENT

Suggested Activities

III. Self care and personal development:
    3. Care of nails:
        a. Demonstrations of scrubbing nails with a brush.
        b. Demonstrations of manicuring nails including use of emery board or nail files, use of manicure scissors, use of orange stick and use of nail polish.
        c. Discussion of importance of keeping nails clean and neatly filed.
        d. Discussion of bad habits in caring for nails such as biting nails and wearing polish that is chipped or cracked, etc.

SELF CARE AND PERSONAL DEVELOPMENT

Content Outlines:

III. Self care and personal development:
  A. Personal appearance:
    4. Care of teeth
      a. Brush teeth regularly
      b. Regular visits to the dentist
    5. Care of hair
      a. Comb hair regularly
      b. Wash hair regularly
      c. Use of oils, tonics, and creams, etc.
      d. Regular visits to barber to have hair cut
      e. Cost of hair cuts for boys
      f. Cost of beauty parlor for girls

SELF CARE AND PERSONAL DEVELOPMENT

Suggested Activities:

III. Self care and personal development:
   A. Personal appearance:
      4. Care of teeth:
         a. Examination of charts and related materials and discussion of why to brush teeth.
         b. Demonstrations of brushing teeth using models as well as actual teeth.
         c. Explanation of use of dental floss, various tooth pastes and powders, soaps and sodas, salt and mouth wash.
         d. View and discuss visual materials pointing out necessity of regular visits to the dentist.
         e. Movies and film strips on care of the teeth.
         f. Field trip to office of a local dentist. Show students office, how to make an appointment with the dentist; have dentist talk on care of the teeth, frequency of visiting the dentist, etc.
      5. Care of hair:
         a. Demonstration and class participation in washing, use of comb and brush, and discussion of how often to clean comb and brush.
         b. Demonstration of washing hair. Discussion and demonstration of how to shampoo with detergents and soaps. Which to purchase.
         c. Discussion of how often to wash hair.
         d. Demonstration and class participation in how to part hair. Discussion of which kind of part would best fit each type of face.
         e. Demonstration of how to set hair using pin curls, curlers or making waves. Discussion of how often hair should be set. Discussion of value of using hair net or scarf to keep hair in place when sleeping.
         f. Demonstration of brushing hair. Discussion of value of brushing hair. Arrange for demonstration and visit to local beauty shop.
         g. Demonstration of home permanents. Discussion of importance of following directions carefully and cautions that must be taken when using home permanent solutions.
         h. Discussion of how often a hair cut is necessary. Where to go for boys and girls. Visit the local barber shop and have someone get a hair cut.
         i. Show visual materials, movies and filmstrips on care of the hair.

SELF CARE AND PERSONAL DEVELOPMENT

Content Outline:

III. Self care and personal development:
    A. Personal appearance:
        6. Care of eyes:
            a. Eye strain
            b. Use of glasses when needed
            c. Have eyes examined regularly
        7. Care of ears:
            a. Do not put objects in ears
            b. Keep ears clean
        8. Care of nose:
            a. Proper blowing of nose
            b. Proper use of handkerchief
            c. Need for clean handkerchief
            d. Do not put objects in the nose
        9. Care of feet:
            a. Have shoes fitted properly
            b. Proper cutting of toe-nails
            c. Flat feet
            d. Ingrown toe-nails
            e. Athlete's foot
            f. Proper drying of feet
            g. Wear clean stockings every day
      10. Toilet habits:
            a. Flush toilet after using
            b. Wash hands after going to toilet

SELF CARE AND PERSONAL DEVELOPMENT

Suggested Activities:

III. Self care and personal development:
    A. Personal appearance:
        6. Care of the eyes:
          a. Discussions on care of the eyes with mention of eye strain, proper use of glasses, regular eye examinations, etc.
          b. Show visual materials on care of the eyes. There are some very good movies about the care of the eyes listed at the end of this unit.
        7. Care of the ears:
          a. Discussions on care of the ears. Point out the dangers of cleaning ears with sharp objects and putting things in the ears.
          b. Show movies and film strips about the care of the ears.
        8. Care of nose:
          a. Discussions on blowing the nose, use of the handkerchief, etc.
          b. Discussions on nose bleeds and other injuries to the nose.
        9. Care of the feet:
          a. Discussions on feet ailments, and the importance of taking proper care of the feet when we are still young so that we will not have foot trouble as we grow older.
          b. Discussions and demonstrations and practise on cutting toenails to prevent ingrown toenails.
          c. Show visual materials on foot ailments such as athlete's foot, ingrown toenails, etc.
          d. Show movies and film strips on the care of the feet. There are some movies on the feet listed at the end of this unit of work.
      10. Toilet habits:
          a. Discussions on toilet habits.

SELF CARE AND PERSONAL DEVELOPMENT

Content Outline:

III. Self care and personal development:
  A. Personal appearance:
    11. Care of clothing:
      a. Protect clothing and keep it clean
        (1) Hang clothing properly when not wearing it
        (2) Wear clean under garments every day
        (3) Keep clothing pressed and neat looking
        (4) Keep clothing repaired and mended
      b. Economical laundering
        (1) Use of laundromats—costs, etc.
        (2) Mend and care for own clothing when possible
        (3) High cost of replacement
      c. Shoe repair
        (1) Regular maintenance cheaper
        (2) Prevent foot trouble
      d. Dry-cleaning
        (1) Cost of dry-cleaning
        (2) Proper care of clothes helps to prevent unnecessary frequency of dry-cleaning and makes them wear longer

SELF CARE AND PERSONAL DEVELOPMENT

Suggested Activities:

III. Self care and personal development:
  A. Personal appearance:
    11. Care of clothing:
      a. Discussion of difference in costs of replacing a garment with a new piece of clothing and protecting and keeping up the appearance of an older garment by regular maintenance (laundering, ironing, dry cleaning, using of, etc.)
      b. Groups may compare various pieces of clothing in newspapers and mail order catalogs.
      c. Demonstrations of the appearance of dirty and torn clothing in various situations. Discussion of what is wrong and needs to be corrected.
      d. Class participation in sewing buttons, sewing seams, darning socks, patching holes, mending tears, pressing pants, and polishing shoes. Personal clothing could be brought to class with the necessary attention being given it.
      e. Show movies on dry-cleaning, laundering and other movies in connection with clothing we wear. Movies and discussions of kinds of cloth used in the making of clothing and how it should be cared for.

SELF CARE AND PERSONAL DEVELOPMENT

Content Outline:

III. Self care and personal development:
  B. Balanced diet—Importance of eating the right kinds of foods:
    1. Basic food groups needed in daily diet:
      a. Dairy foods
      b. Meat groups
      c. Vegetables and fruits
      d. Breads and cereals
      e. Other foods
    2. Nutrients found in the above groups:
      a. Minerals
      b. Proteins
      c. Vitamins
      d. Carbohydrates
      e. Fats

SELF CARE AND PERSONAL DEVELOPMENT

Suggested Activities:

III. Self care and personal development:
  B. Balanced diet—Importance of eating the right kinds of foods:
    1. Discussion of importance of establishing good eating habits with three meals a day at regular intervals—plus between meal lunches.
    2. Have some understanding of basic seven food groups so the individual will be able to understand what kinds of foods and how much should comprise his daily diet. Use visual materials.
    3. Discussion of importance of breakfast—include planning of well proportioned breakfast and preparing of good breakfast to be eaten in the classroom.
    4. Planning of adequate noon meals whether they are to be a carried lunch, a counter snack or dinner.
    5. Planning of well proportioned evening meals. An example of a snack, lunch or dinner can be planned, prepared and served with discussion of how various foods included help our bodies.
    6. Discussion of adequate between meal lunches.
    7. Dramatise a situation in which the students order a meal in a restaurant. Let some students be the waiters and waitresses, and let others be the customers giving them an opportunity of ordering meals which include the right kinds of food.
    8. Prepare foods in the classroom and discuss the food nutrients in each food prepared.
    9. Take field trip to a nearby restaurant, and give the students an opportunity to order a meal in a restaurant choosing the right kinds of food, and letting them have an opportunity of paying for the food they buy so that they have the opportunity of observing the cost, etc.
    10. Show movies and film strips about foods and their nutrients, preparing foods, buying foods, planning meals, etc. There are some good movies about the above listed at the end of this unit.

SELF CARE AND PERSONAL DEVELOPMENT

Content Outline:

III. Self care and personal development:
    C. Importance of other factors contributing to good health:
        1. Good posture
            a. Stand straight
            b. Sit straight
            c. Effects of posture on other organs and proper functioning of the body
        2. Fresh air and exercise
            a. Need for daily exercise and fresh air
            b. Proper kinds of exercises for various age groups
            c. Need for proper conditioning for certain types of exercise before full participation
            d. Proper dress for seasonal and type of exercise
            e. Affects of weather and climate on types of exercise
            f. Need for sufficient rest—(1) at least 8 hours per day
        3. Care of illnesses and ailments
            a. Take care of all illnesses and ailments
            b. Common illnesses and ailments
            c. Physical examinations
                (1) How often?
                (2) Where?
                (3) Often required for employment
                    (a) Source (City Hall, Company Doctor, Family Doctor)
                (4) T.B. check up (free mobile unit)
        4. Mental hygiene
            a. Effects of personality on health
            b. Getting along with people—social know how

SELF CARE AND PERSONAL DEVELOPMENT

Suggested Activities:

III. Self care and personal development:
    C. Importance of other factors contributing to good health:
        1. Demonstrations of good and bad posture. Class participation in correct ways of sitting, standing and walking.
        2. Constant checking of posture in full length mirror.
        3. Viewing and discussion of visual materials on posture.
        4. Discussion of importance of good posture to appearance and health.
        5. Discussion of affect of good posture on other organs of the body.
        6. Some form of checking may be used to cover all aspects of personal appearance. Make use of charts.
        7. Discussion of importance of proper rest with the correct number of hours for rest each night pointing out that some individuals need more rest than others. Also, include the fresh air factor in getting sufficient rest.
        8. Discussions on the need for fresh air and exercise pointing out the proper kinds of exercise for various age groups, the need for proper conditioning for certain types of exercise before full participation, the proper dress for seasonal and different types of exercise, and the effects of weather and climate on types of exercise needed.
        9. Show movies and film strips on fresh air, rest, posture, exercise, etc. There are movies on these subjects listed at the end of this unit.
      10. Discussion of the most common ailments and what should be done for them. Some of these ailments include: colds, headache, open sores, scratches, cuts, tired muscles, stomach aches, etc.
      11. Persistence of any ailment should have medical attention.
      12. Discussion of who to go to when illness or ailment occurs with emphasis on company doctor or nurse. Necessity for periodic physical examination.
      13. Practice on being able to tell what is wrong with you.
      14. View and discuss visual materials.
      15. Show movies and film strips on common ailments and illnesses listed above.

SELF CARE AND PERSONAL DEVELOPMENT

Content Outline:

III. Self care and personal development:
    D. Importance of courtesy and good manners—Respect for others:
        1. Table manners:
            a. Setting the table
            b. Table customs
            c. Speed in eating
            d. The napkin
            e. The family attitude
            f. Chewing food
            g. Removing food from the mouth
            h. Accidents at table
        2. Personal manners:
            a. Picking
            b. Expectorating (spitting)
            c. Offensive odors
            d. Obscene language
            e. Personal remarks
            f. Personal comparisons
            g. Personal questions
            h. Bathroom manners
            i. Use of handkerchief
        3. Group manners:
            a. Shaking hands
            b. Burping and belching
            c. The sniffer and the snorter
            d. Use of make-up in public
            e. Chewing gum
            f. Smoking
            g. Loud talking
            h. When to say thank you
            i. When to say please
            j. When to say pardon me

SELF CARE AND PERSONAL DEVELOPMENT

Suggested Activities:

III. Self care and personal developments:
    D. Importance of courtesy and good manners—Respect for others:
        1. Table manners:
            a. Make use of a model set table where the following demonstrations and discussions can be carried out:
                (1) Proper holding and use of knife, fork and spoon
                (2) Proper use of napkin
                (3) When to say please, thank you, excuse or pardon me
                (4) Ask to please pass food—do not reach
                (5) Proper way to chew food—eat with mouth closed
                (6) Speed of eating—eat slowly and do not gulp food
                (7) Proper handling of accidents at the table
                (8) Men wait for ladies to be seated—help with chairs
                (9) Ask to be excused from the table before leaving
              (10) Discussion of proper table talk (a group planned meal served with all good table manners observed and carried through)
            b. View and discuss visual materials.
            c. Set up real situations—what would you do?
            d. Visit the local restaurant where manners observed in the classroom can be put into practice.
        2. Personal Manners: 3. Group manners: 4. Conduct in public places:
            a. Courtesy and respect for others—
                (1) Discussion of addressing people correctly (Miss, Mrs., Mr., Sir, etc.)
                (2) Discussion of responding to and listening to directions
                (3) Discussion of importance of accepting major decisions
                (4) Discussion of fact that most people are anxious to help and do not criticize unjustly
                (5) View and discuss visual materials—don't interrupt when others are speaking
                (6) Use of thank you, you are welcome, pardon or excuse me, etc. Demonstrations and discussions of various occasions you would use these expressions of courtesy

SELF CARE AND PERSONAL DEVELOPMENT

Content Outline:

III. Self care and personal development:
    D. Importance of courtesy and good manners—Respect for others:
        4. Conduct in public places:
            a. At a hotel
            b. At the theater
            c. At a movie
            d. At church
            e. In school
            f. In the library
            g. In the street car or bus
            h. In the automobile—on automobile trips
            i. On trains
            j. In the restaurant

SELF CARE AND PERSONAL DEVELOPMENT

Suggested Activities:

III. Self care and personal development:
    D. Importance of courtesy and good manners—Respect for others:
       2. Personal manners: 3. Group manners: 4. Conduct in Public
                                places: (cont'd)
        b. Proper conversation
          (1) Discussion of proper topics of conversation pointing out that it should be cheerful and about subjects of general interest to all
          (2) Emphasize that unpleasant topics and pointed remarks about people in the group create unfriendliness
          (3) Point out that profanity, obscenity and suggestive talk only show lack of judgment and training
          (4) Discuss what topics are not proper for conversation and why. Examples: What may have occurred in the institution; what your employer says or is doing (carrying tales), all about your boy or girl friends
          (5) Set up situations that provide opportunities for proper conversation and allow for practice under varying circumstances.
        c. Have discussions and show visual materials and set up examples about all of the manners listed in the content outline under personal manners, group manners, and conduct in public places. Show movies and film strips listed at the end of this unit that apply to these subjects.

SELF CARE AND PERSONAL DEVELOPMENT

Content Outline:

III. Self care and personal development:
   E. Importance of having respect for equipment, property and the rights of others:
      1. Personal:
         a. Price in ownership
         b. Keep things looking nice
         c. Reflects your habits
      2. Living quarters:
         a. What is needed for room, apartment, etc.
         b. How to set it up
         c. Room maintenance
      3. Public:
         a. For the use of all
         b. All have share in the cost
         c. All must protect

SELF CARE AND PERSONAL DEVELOPMENT

Suggested Activities:

III. Self care and personal development:
  E. Importance of having respect for equipment, property and the rights of others:
   1. Personal property:
     a. Discussions on what personal property do you own. Answer the questions: How do you take care of it? What condition is it in? Can you replace it?
     b. Have each person bring an article of his personal possessions to class for examination and discussion. What kind of person owns this article?
     c. Discussion with emphasis on fact that all property lasts longer and becomes less expensive in up keep when taken care of, thereby making it possible to purchase other articles.
     d. Demonstration that articles that are slightly damaged can be repaired rather than replaced. Point out that you will have to pay the bill.
     e. Trips to home furnishing stores. Use and discuss various home magazines.
   2. Public property:
     a. Take a walk around the institution pointing out different forms of public or "state" property.
     b. Discussion on where it comes from and who pays the original and cost of maintenance.
     c. Show how articles can be repaired when only slightly damaged and that this is cheaper than buying new articles.
     d. Make use of newspapers and mail order or manufacturers catalogs to show the current cost of equipment.
     e. Discussion on the fact that you will be paying for public property as soon as you become a worker and wage earner, and that you are taking care of your own investment when you take proper care of public property.
     f. Show and discuss visual materials.

SELF CARE AND PERSONAL DEVELOPMENT

Suggested Source Materials to Be Used in This Unit on:

Self Care and Personal Development:

A. Movies:

1.	*How Clean Is Clean*	American Gas Company
2.	*The Clean Look*	Modern No. 150
3.	*Kitty Cleans Up*	Wisconsin State Board of Health
4.	*Scrub Game*	Modern No. 21
5.	*Your Cleanliness*	Wisconsin State Board of Health
6.	*About Faces*	United States Public Health Service
7.	*Personal Hygiene for Boys*	Wisconsin State Board of Health
8.	*Molly Grows Up*	Wisconsin State Board of Health
9.	*50,000 Lives*	Association Films, Inc.
10.	*Color of Health*	American Bakers Association
11.	*Modern Guide to Health*	Wisconsin State Board of Health
12.	*Lease on Life*	Wisconsin State Board of Health
13.	*Fitness Is a Family Affair*	Wisconsin State Board of Health
14.	*Loosing to Win*	Modern No. 1120
15.	*Fresh Air for Health*	Sante Fe Film Bureau
16.	*It's Your Health*	Wisconsin State Board of Health
17.	*For Health and Happiness*	Wisconsin State Board of Health
18.	*Life of a Healthy Child*	Wisconsin State Board of Health
19.	*Fly Control Through Basic Sanitation*	Communicable Disease Center
20.	*Denny's Dental Date*	Wisconsin State Board of Health
21.	*Swab Your Choppers*	Wisconsin State Board of Health
22.	*Judy's Smile*	Wisconsin State Board of Health
23.	*Our Teeth*	Wisconsin State Board of Health
24.	*The Seeing Eye*	The Seeing Eye, Incorporated
25.	*The Vision Makers*	Better Vision Institute
26.	*Magic of Vision*	Better Vision Institute
27.	*The Walking Machine*	American Food Can Institute, Inc.
28.	*The Foot and Its Problems*	American Podiatry Association
29.	*Shake Hands With Your Feet*	American Podiatry Association
30.	*Border Weave*	Wool Bureau Incorporated
31.	*Co-op Wool From Fleece to Fabric*	Farm Credit Districts
32.	*Uncle Henry Saves the Play*	Modern Talking Picture Service
33.	*Food Preparation*	Communicable Disease Center
34.	*Fresh From the West*	Union Pacific Railway
35.	*The Son Goes North*	Modern No. 161
36.	*Food That Builds Good Health*	Wisconsin State Board of Health
37.	*Story of Oats and Oatmeal*	Modern No. 562
38.	*Magic Cup*	Modern No. 1008
39.	*Crackers by the Billion*	Modern No. 527
40.	*Beef and Carving*	
41.	*Something You Didn't Eat*	Wisconsin State Board of Health
42.	*Mealtime Can Be a Happy Time*	Wisconsin State Board of Health

SELF CARE AND PERSONAL DEVELOPMENT

Suggested Source Materials to Be Used in This Unit on:

Self Care and Personal Development:

A. Movies:

43.	*Vitamin Rivers*	Modern No. 345
44.	*Milk Parade*	Wisconsin State Board of Health
45.	*Citrus Contributions Fresh for Health*	Modern No. 1142
46.	*Rainbow Harvest*	Modern No. 110
47.	*Treasure Islands*	Modern No. 78
48.	*Good Food—Good Health—Good Looks*	Modern No. 490
49.	*All Flesh Is Grass*	American Cattlemen's Association
50.	*American Harvest*	General Motors
51.	*Beef Maker*	Modern No. 557
52.	*A Nation's Meat*	Swift & Company
53.	*Green Giant's Magic*	Modern No. 514
54.	*Cows, Milk, and America*	Modern No. 1182
55.	*Adventures in Dairy Land*	Modern No. 1153
56.	*Along the Milky Way*	Union Pacific Railroad
57.	*Judy Learns About Milk*	Wisconsin State Board of Health
58.	*How Do You Stand*	Wisconsin State Board of Health
59.	*Circulation of the Blood*	American Heart Association
60.	*Fun That Builds Good Health*	Wisconsin State Board of Health
61.	*Sleep—It's Wonderful*	Modern No. 727
62.	*First Aid I*	American Red Cross
63.	*First Aid II*	American Red Cross
64.	*Insects as Carriers of Disease*	
65.	*Defense Against Invasion*	Wisconsin State Board of Health
66.	*How Disease Travels*	Wisconsin State Board of Health
67.	*What Is Disease*	Wisconsin State Board of Health
68.	*Common Cold*	Wisconsin State Board of Health
69.	*How to Catch a Cold*	Association Films, Inc.
70.	*Confessions of a Cold*	Wisconsin State Board of Health
71.	*Sniffles and Sneezes*	Wisconsin State Board of Health
72.	*Let's Have Fewer Colds*	Wisconsin State Board of Health
73.	*Are You Popular*	Roa's Films
74.	*Acts of Courtesy*	Roa's Films
75.	*It Takes All Kinds*	Wisconsin State Board of Health
76.	*Friendship Begins at Home*	Roa's Films
77.	*As Your Home Goes*	Modern No. 1101
78.	*How to Raise a Boy*	Du Pont
79.	*Faith in Boys*	General Motors
80.	*Mr. Finley's Feelings*	Metropolitan Life
81.	*Control Your Emotions*	Roa's Films
82.	*O'Mara's Chain Miracle*	General Motors
83.	*Ford People*	Ford Motor Company

SELF CARE AND PERSONAL DEVELOPMENT

Suggested Source Materials to Be Used in This Unit on:

Self Care and Personal Development:

B. Pamphlets, Posters, Charts, Etc.

Teachers Guide to Free Curr. Materials	Educators Progress Service
Learning to Cook and Serve Our Meals	National Dairy Council
Everyday Care and Good Food for Sound Teeth	National Dairy Council
A Guide to Good Eating	National Dairy Council
Grin or Grouch	National Dairy Council
Fit for Fun	National Dairy Council
Postures on Parade	National Dairy Council
Eat a Square Lunch	National Dairy Council
Dick's Plan and How It Grew	Wheat Flour Inst.
Our Daily Food	American Institute of Baking
Which Are You	General Mills
Ways to Keep Well and Happy	American T.B. League
Beauty on a Budget	Gillette Safety Razor
Click With the Crowd	Bristol Meyers
Coach Calls the Signals	Bristol Meyers
Get on the Beam	Bristol Meyers
How Do You Rate Chart	Bristol Meyers
Jane's Diary	Bristol Meyers
Tales Your Hands Tell	Bristol Meyers
Be Proud of Your Hands	Bristol Meyers
Rate With Your Date	Bristol Meyers
Grooming for the Job	Bristol Meyers
Grooming for School	Bristol Meyers
Perspiring Is Healthful	Bristol Meyers
Misc. Washing and Bathing	Bristol Meyers and Lever Bros.
How Do You Do and Others	McKnight and McKnight

C. Slide Films:

Your Posture Good or Bad	School Library
Your Skin	School Library
Dressing Well Is a Game	Household Finance Inc.
Suzie Makes a Dress	Bates Fabrics Inc.
Manners Make a Difference	School Library
You and Your Clothes	Photo-art Visual Service
Before It Is Too Late (dental)	Zurich-Amer. Ins. Co.

D. Books:

Health Stories, Care of Hair, Table Manners, Food Habits	Scott Foreman
Exploring in Science, Gardens, Vitamins, Plants and Animals Help Us	Ginn and Company

GETTING AND KEEPING A JOB

Objectives:

1. To give pupils a *realistic* concept of the kinds of jobs they will be able to get.
2. To make pupils aware of the qualifications they must have to get and keep these jobs.
3. To develop the right attitudes and work habits to obtain and hold these jobs and be successful in the work world.

Content Outline:

IV. Getting and keeping a job:
  A. Employment services—Getting the job:
    1. What jobs are available—Kinds of jobs for the mentally retarded.
      —Farm work
      —Restaurants and Cafeterias
      —Janitor work
      —Hospital work of different kinds
      —Bakeries
      —Laundry
      —Cleaners
      —Housekeeping; baby-sitting, etc.
      —Factories
      —Shoe shops
      —Shoe shining in barber shops
      —Gardeners—care takers—lawn work
      —Pin-setters (extra pocket money)
      —Ushers
      —Bell boys—bell hops
      —Gas station work
      —Construction work of various kinds
      —Work for sanitation department
        a. Garbage Collectors
        b. Street Cleaners
      —Stock boys in department stores
      —Meat packing plants
      —Etc., Unskilled labor

GETTING AND KEEPING A JOB

Suggested Activities:

IV. Getting and keeping a job:
    A. Employment services—Getting the job:
        1. What jobs are available—Kinds of jobs for the mentally retarded.
            a. Have pupils make a list of jobs they think they can get—seatwork.
            b. Put the list on board and have them copy all jobs they can think of as a group.
            c. Class discussion on each job mentioned—what kind of work involved, etc.
            d. Field trips to a laundry, hospital, bakery, restaurant, and factory to see the people at work in the jobs discussed and to talk to the personnel managers about the job benefits, etc.
            e. Movies on as many of the above listed jobs as possible.
            f. Film strips on jobs in restaurant, grocery stores, gas stations from Eyegate Visuals Aids Company.

GETTING AND KEEPING A JOB

Content Outline:

IV. Getting and keeping a job:
    A. Employment services—Getting the job:
        2. Qualifications necessary—Work habits and attitudes—What employers look for:
           a. Punctuality
           b. Honesty
           c. Cooperation
           d. Dependability—reliability
           e. Perseverance
           f. Interest in work
           g. Courtesy
           h. Ability to take criticism
           i. Ability to do the work
           j. Ability to follow directions
           k. Loyalty
           l. Self control
           m. Cleanliness
           n. Consideration for others
           o. Health

GETTING AND KEEPING A JOB

Suggested Activities:

IV. Getting and keeping a job:
  A. Employment services—Getting the job:
    2. Qualifications necessary—Work habits and attitudes—What employers look for:
      a. Class discussion on work habits and attitudes.
      b. Class discussion on qualities and abilities needed for each job mentioned above and in their lists.
      c. Field trips listed above are part of this work.
      d. Read and discuss pamphlets from the Employment Bureau.
      e. Make bulletin board and charts from these pamphlets illustrating the information found in them.
      f. Socio-drama on different characterizations of various personality types seeking jobs using the students in the class (also charts and pictures).
      g. MOVIES:
        It Takes All Kinds
        Acts of Courtesy
        Are You Popular
        Friendship Begins at Home
        Control Your Emotions
        As Your Home Goes
        The American Customer
        Behind Each Sale

GETTING AND KEEPING A JOB

Objectives:

1. To teach pupils how to go about finding a job and the services that are available to aid him find employment. Pupils must learn how to use the services that are available.
2. To inform pupils about unions and their regulations and limitations.

Content Outline:

IV. Getting and keeping a job:
   A. Employment services—Getting the job:
      3. How to find a job—Services available:
         a. Employment Bureau
         b. Classified ads in newspapers
         c. Friends and acquaintances who might be helpful
         d. Help wanted signs in windows of businesses and industries
         e. Use of the telephone to help get a job
         f. Going for an interview
         g. How to fill out application blanks
      4. Union regulations:
         a. The closed shop
         b. The open shop
         c. Union fees
         d. Union Restrictions
         e. Union meetings, etc.
         f. Strikes

GETTING AND KEEPING A JOB

Suggested Activities:

IV. Getting and keeping a job:
   A. Employment services—Getting the job:
      3. How to find a job—Services available:
         a. Look up classified ads for obtaining jobs in the newspapers.
         b. Make "Help Wanted" ads like ones they might see in windows of business places and industry.
         c. Class discussions about all of this material.
         d. Movies and film strips on "The Job Interview."
         e. Practice calling to make inquiries on telephone using teletrainer kit.
         f. Practice having job interviews in the classroom. (Socio-drama)
         g. Use cartoon charts on the job interview.
         h. Learn vocabulary of the application blanks:
           —flash cards
           —blackboard drills
           —vocabulary games
         i. Use the big teacher-and-pupil made poster-paper chart in color for instruction on filling out application blanks. Use the bulletin board for display purposes. Fill out real applications.
         j. End part C with a field trip to the Employment Bureau. Have one pupil interviewed and sent through the employment bureau just as though he were really seeking a job; then discuss the the results.
      4. Union Regulations:
         a. Discussion of what unions are.
         b. Discussion about advantages and disadvantages.
         c. Have a union representative come to speak to pupils in the classroom.
         d. Discuss the union with each of the personnel managers we meet on our field trips listed above.
         e. Movies and film strips about unions.
         f. Make charts illustrating the advantages and disadvantages of unions.

GETTING AND KEEPING A JOB

Objectives:

1. To prepare pupils to budget time so they can get to work and be punctual.
2. To teach student how to find his work location.
3. To inform student of methods of transportation that can be used to get to work.

Content Outline:

IV. Getting and keeping a job:
- B. Time for work:
  1. What time do I have to get up in the morning?
     How much sleep is necessary?
     a. Time to be at work
     b. Setting the alarm clock
     c. Amount of time necessary to get to the job.
     d. Allow time to dress, eat, and prepare for lunch
- C. Location and direction:
  1. Which way shall I go?
     a. Street name and building number
     b. North, South, East, West

GETTING AND KEEPING A JOB

Suggested activities:

IV. Getting and keeping a job:
   B. Time for work:
      1. What time do I have to get up in the morning?
      How much sleep is necessary?
         a. Demonstration and discussion of how to tell time with continued practice.
         b. Demonstration on how to wind and set alarm clocks. Practice setting the alarm for specific times.
         c. Discuss differences in time going to work between city and country.
         d. Select various points and estimate the time necessary to get there.
         e. Follow up with actual measurement.
         f. Estimate time necessary for bathing, dressing, eating, and preparing a lunch. Measure the actual time by completion of these tasks in actual classroom practice.
   C. Location and direction:
      1. Which way shall I go?
         a. Discuss location and directions of various buildings and points of interest.
         b. Assign house numbers to institution buildings and then practice giving their locations and finding them.
         c. Practice locating various points in nearby community after class discussion.

GETTING AND KEEPING A JOB

Content Outline:

IV. Getting and keeping a job:
  D. Transportation:
    1. How shall I get to work?
      a. Walk
      b. Bus
      c. Taxi
      d. Street car
      e. Train
      f. Ride with friends
    2. What must I know?
      (1) Schedule of Bus or Street Car
      a. Location of stop
      b. Proper change for fare
      c. Actions on bus
      d. Where to get off (going and coming)
      e. How to make the bus stop
      f. Buying a newspaper (name, where, price)
    3. What can I observe?
      a. Traffic (safety rules)
      b. Signals (vehicles and pedestrians)
      c. Street signs
    4. If I get lost, what shall I do?
      a. Look for a policeman
      b. Ask bus driver or street car motorman for directions
      c. Speak to a pedestrian

GETTING AND KEEPING A JOB

Suggested Activities:

IV. Getting and keeping a job:
    D. Transportation:
        1. How shall I get to work?
            a. Discuss various forms of transportation in both urban and rural areas. Consider cost, convenience and most direct route.
            b. Classroom discussion and practice in imaginary transportation situations making use of visual materials and emphasizing the things to know.
            c. Obtain samples of bus tokens, transfers, car tickets, etc., and discuss their use.
        2. What must I know?
        3. What can I observe?
        4. If I get lost, what shall I do?
            a. Demonstrate characteristics of most common public transportation by *actual use* in nearby communities and check time factors.
            b. Field trip to nearby city to use city bus transportation, learn to transfer from one bus to the other, etc.
            c. Field trip to nearby city to ride on the elevated and subway trains. Transfer to city bus using transfer slip issued by conductor of train.
            d. View visual materials on safety and discuss traffic regulations and safety rules.
            e. Use samples of different signs such as "STOP, PEDESTRIAN CROSSING, NO LOITERING," etc., and practice following safety rules in a variety of situations. Observe and practice safety regulations in nearby communities.
            f. Discuss and demonstrate what to do when lost. Who to ask for directions, and what to tell such a person.
            g. Have policeman come to class and talk about how they can help you in various situations.
            h. Visit the police station after such a speech to learn of safety facilities of the community.
            i. Use safety pamphlets from the local community safety office as a basis for class discussion, and make posters illustrating the material in the pamphlets. Use this material for bulletin board display.
            j. Practice counting exact change for fare.

GETTING AND KEEPING A JOB

Objectives:

1. To teach pupils how to use a map.
2. To teach pupils how to prepare a lunch to take to work with them.

Content Outline:

IV. Getting and keeping a job:
    E. Use of maps
        1. City maps:
            a. Location of home (street name and number)
            b. Location of work
            c. Public transportation routes
        2. State maps:
            a. Location of city
        3. National maps:
            a. Location of state

GETTING AND KEEPING A JOB

Suggested Activities:

IV. Getting and keeping a job:
   E. Use of maps
      1. City maps
      2. State maps
      3. National maps
         a. Examine various types of maps in class, and locate familiar places (local, state, national transportation).
         b. Pick out specific locations and have pupils trace the streets or highways to be taken to reach the location.
         c. View and discuss films and other visual materials.
         d. Make a map of the institution grounds or community and locate various points of interest.
         e. Discuss the source and cost of different kinds of maps.

GETTING AND KEEPING A JOB

Objectives:

1. To teach pupils when and how to go out to buy a lunch. (Also where)
2. To teach pupils proper manners when eating in public places.
3. To teach pupils how to read a menu in a public eating place.

Content Outline:

IV. Getting and keeping a job:
    F. Best method of eating lunch:
       (dependent upon individual situation and needs)
       1. Carry lunch:
          a. What do I want to take?
             (1) Bulk
             (2) Price
          b. Cost
             (1) Right kinds of food
             (2) Enough to eat
             (3) Adequate daily budget
          c. Where can I get it?
             (1) Grocery store
             (2) Meat market
             (3) Fruit store
             (4) Super market
          d. Lunch schedule
             (1) When do I go?
             (2) How long do I stay?

GETTING AND KEEPING A JOB

Suggested Activities:

IV. Getting and keeping a job:
  F. Best method of eating lunch:
     (dependent upon individual situation and needs)
     1. Carry lunch:
        (Obtain samples of proper utensils for carrying lunch and discuss
        and demonstrate their use and proper care. These will include
        lunch pail, thermos bottles, napkins, wax paper, or sandwich bags,
        and salt and pepper shakers.)
        a. Discussion of what makes an adequate lunch. What are the
           different kinds of stores, and what do they specialize in? Prac-
           tice in purchasing in school room store.
        b. Compile a list of various lunch menus and make field trip to
           the local stores. Purchase appropriate lunch foods demonstrat-
           ing how to make selections and method of payment.
        c. Discussion of stores visited as to quantity of foods available,
           prices shown, and quality of the merchandise.
        d. Prepare actual lunches to include making sandwiches, wrapping
           lunch, preparing beverage, and packing the lunch pail. Keep
           track of cost and work out an adequate daily budget.
        e. Discussion on lunch schedules as to length and when they
           usually occur.

GETTING AND KEEPING A JOB

Content Outline:

IV. Getting and keeping a job:
   F. Best method of eating lunch:
     (dependent upon individual situation and needs)
     2. Buying lunch:
       a. Where do I go?
         (1) Plant cafeteria
         (2) Drug store
         (3) Short orders
         (4) Traveling vendors
         (5) Restaurant
         (6) Drive-in
       b. What must I know?
         (1) Differences in the above
         (2) Menu
         (3) Cost of items
         (4) How to order
         (5) Where to eat the food
         (6) Do I get enough
         (7) What do I do with the dirty dishes
         (8) Where and how much to pay

GETTING AND KEEPING A JOB

Suggested Activities:

IV. Getting and keeping a job:
   F. Best method of eating lunch:
     (dependent upon individual situation and needs)
     2. Buying lunch:
       a. Discussion on various types of eating establishments. Point out advantages and disadvantages of each.
       b. Present demonstration on how to eat in each of the types listed.
       c. Survey costs and work out a daily budget that will provide an adequate diet. Gather menus and compare costs.
       d. Set up situation that might be found in different eating establishments, and give boys and girls chance to show what they would do.
       e. Develop vocabulary found on the menu. Use various vocabulary building games, flash cards, charts, and black board.
       f. Show movies on right kinds of foods to eat.
           Citrus Contributions to Flesh for Health
           The King Who Came to Breakfast
           Good Food—Good Health—Good Looks
           American Harvest
       g. Have Homemaking Teacher serve a meal and practice our table manners.
       h. Take field trips into the community and visit various types of eating places discussed. Order and eat a meal in a restaurant. (Practice ordering meals in the classroom first.) Have pupils pay their own bills.

GETTING AND KEEPING A JOB

Objectives:

1. To teach pupils what a vacation is for; how it can be used; and how to plan for the time and cost.

Content Outline:

IV. Getting and keeping a job:
    G. How to use vacation time:
        1. Cost of vacation:
            a. Will determine what can be done.
            b. Should be saved for and paid at the time.
        2. Type of vacation:
            a. Travel
                (1) Train
                (2) Car
                (3) Bus
                (4) Plane
            b. Stay at home
                (1) Time for rest and relaxation
                (2) Catch up on various tasks
            c. Visit relations and friends
                (1) Renew old acquaintances
                (2) Don't stay too long and wear out your welcome
                (3) Pay your own expenses
                (4) Don't take advantage of your host and hostess

GETTING AND KEEPING A JOB

Suggested Activities:

IV. Getting and keeping a job:
   G. How to use vacation time:
   1. Cost of vacation:
      a. Discussion on when vacations can be taken.
      b. Discuss what each student feels he would like to do during his leisure time, and where these activities might be carried out.
      c. Discuss the cost of the various things that can be done, and how one must plan and budget for this expense long in advance.
      d. Discuss length of vacation and how it limits what can be done.
   2. Type of vacation:
      a. Show movies on vacations such as:
         Canyon Country—Ford Motor Company
         Yellowstone—Ford Motor Company
         West to the Tetons—Ford Motor Company
         Fishing for Fun—General Motors
         What a Vacation—Ford Motor Company
      b. Show teacher's slides taken on various vacations.
      c. Discuss staying at home and relaxing or getting various tasks done that you didn't have time to do before.
      d. Class discussion including things listed on outline.

THE FAMILY

Objectives:

1. To help students acquire an understanding of the responsibilities of the various members of a family unit.
2. To develop an understanding of the members that constitute the family unit.
3. To acquaint the students with the problems and responsibilities involved in setting up a family and home.
4. To acquaint the students with the privileges of family life that can be enjoyed only as a member of a family.
5. To acquaint the students with financial and business matters pertaining to family life—facts about meeting needs and acquiring the necessities and luxuries of life.
6. To acquaint the students with the possibilities for developing spiritual and recreational activities within the family unit which enrich the lives of each member of the family and bind the members of a family into a closer unit.

Content Outline:

V. The family: (parents, children, relatives)
  A. The family unit:
    1. Members of the family
      a. Immediate family in household
        (1) parents (or guardians)
        (2) siblings
          —Brothers
          —Sisters
          —Half and step brothers and sisters
      b. Other relatives
        (1) Grandparents
        (2) Aunts and uncles
        (3) Cousins
        (4) Etc.

THE FAMILY

Suggested Activities

V. The family
A. The family unit:
1. Discussion regarding what a family is. Who or what makes up a family unit? Bring out that it takes the cooperation of all members to make a happy family. Children as well as adults have responsibilities.
2. Discussion of responsibilities of individual members of the family.
3. Play guessing games, identifying family members by descriptions of that member's role or responsibility in a family.
4. Discussion on family customs. Have each member of class tell about some family customs in their families.
5. Show pictures of families, discuss what they are doing.

THE FAMILY

Content Outline:

V. The family: (Cont'd)
    B. Parents responsibilities and role in family unit:
        1. Provide love and companionship.
        2. Provide material needs.
            a. Shelter—home—place to live
            b. Clothing
            c. Food
            d. Etc.
        3. Provide spiritual development and religious training.
        4. Provide educational experiences and opportunities.
        5. Provide recreational opportunities and social development.
        6. Teach children democratic living.
        7. Teach children consideration for others—manners and courtesy.
        8. Provide healthy living conditions, and teach children proper health habits.
        9. Mother's role.
            a. Homemaker
            b. Care for children
            c. Sometimes helps husband in role as provider
      10. Father's role.
            a. Provider
            b. Help wife in role as homemaker and care of children
    C. Children's responsibilities and role in the family unit:
        1. Share in home tasks.
        2. Understand and respect authority of parents.
        3. Cooperate in family duties and responsibilities.
        4. Adjust to family income and needs.
        5. Understand family customs.
        6. Sometimes—help to earn money.

THE FAMILY

Suggested Activities

V. The family: (Cont'd)
  B. Parents responsibilities and role in family unit:
    1. Class discussion on responsibilities of parents to their family—Discuss all points listed in the content outline of parents responsibilities.
    2. Discussion regarding the effects on the family when parents do not take care of these responsibilities. Point out that men and women should not marry until they are mature enough and ready to provide these responsibilities.
    3. Have students make a list of all the responsibilities they can think of for which parents are responsible.
    4. Have students make a list of as many of the material needs— (necessities) as they can think of that must be provided by the parents.
    5. Discuss students own futures and point out that if they have families they must meet these responsibilities.
    6. Show movies on parents providing some of these responsibilities:
        Insects as Carriers of Disease—
        Fly Control Through Basic Sanitation—
        *Two Cheers for Charlie—*Sterling Movies, Inc.
        *Friendship Begins at Home—*Modern
        *As Your Home Goes—*Modern
        *Fitness Is a Family Affair—*Wisconsin State Board of Health
        *How to Raise a Boy—*DuPont or Farm Film Foundation
  C. Children's responsibilities and role in the family unit:
    1. Discussion of all points under content outline regarding Children's responsibilities in the homes.
    2. Use socio-drama to help pupils gain insight into situations that might occur in the home adjustment between parents and children, and between siblings.

THE FAMILY

Content Outline:

V. The family: (Cont'd)
    D. Family finances:
        1. Sources of family income
            a. Salary or wages from a job
            b. Owning a business
            c. Renting property owned by family
            d. Selling services to others
            e. Investments, dividends, and interests, etc.
            f. Social Welfare
        2. Family expenses
            a. Shelter
                (1) House payments
                (2) Rent
                (3) Taxes
                (4) Maintenance
                (5) Depreciation
            b. Food
            c. Clothing
            d. Medical, dental and health expenses
            e. Insurances
                (1) Hospitalization
                (2) Life
                (3) Sickness and accident
                (4) Car insurance
                (5) Personal property
                (6) Etc.
            f. Utilities
            g. Taxes
            h. Education
            i. Transportation
            j. Church
            k. Recreation
            l. Club Membership and Membership in other organizations
            m. Savings—
                (1) Bank accounts
                (2) Savings bonds
                (3) Postal
                (4) Investments, etc.

THE FAMILY

Suggested Activities

V. The family: (Cont'd)
  D. Family finances:
     1. Discussion on sources of family income, pointing out how the family can make the money that is necessary to meet the needs of family.
     2. Discussion on family expenses:
        The cost of shelter depending on what type of shelter one seeks. Cost of maintenance, etc.
     3. Discussion about cost of food and clothing.
     4. Discussion on cost of utilities needs in the home.
     5. Discussion on cost of medical and dental expenses for a family of several members.
     6. Discussion about the kinds of insurances needed by every family, and the cost of these insurances.
        It should be brought to the attention of the students that some of these insurances are a necessity for the protection and welfare of the family in the event of an emergency.
     7. Have students make lists of things other members of the family besides the father can do to help earn income for the family.
     8. Discussion on how each member of the family can save the family money. Point out that if parents are going to provide adequately for the family, they must have the cooperation of the whole family.
     9. Make scrap books illustrating how family members can earn money, and ways of saving money, along with efficient management.
     10. Discussions on job experiences that members of the class have had. Have them tell about their various work experiences, and discuss things that were learned from these experiences.
     11. Discuss occupations of students' fathers and mothers.

THE FAMILY

Content Outline:

V. The family: (Cont'd)
  D. Family finances:
    3. Responsibility for family spending
      a. In our culture—father's over-all responsibility
      b. Each member in family has a responsibility to adjust to family income in terms of his needs in relationship to other family needs.
    4. Clothing for the family
      a. New clothing
        (1) Needs
        (2) Costs
      b. Maintenance of Clothing
        (1) Proper care—saves in costs and keeps clothes looking nicer—longer
        (2) Costs
          —Cleaning
          —Storage
          —Sewing, etc.
      c. Study of wardrobe for men and women
        (1) What clothes are needed for cold, hot, and stormy weather
        (2) What is needed for dress-up occasions
          (a) Parties
          (b) Sunday
          (c) Special occasions
        (3) What under clothing is needed
          (a) Kinds
          (b) Care
          (c) Amount
        (4) What night clothes are needed
          (a) Kind
          (b) Care
    5. Food for the family
      a. What to consider in buying food
        (1) What is needed in daily diet
          (a) Basic food groups
            —Dairy foods
            —Meat group
            —Vegetables and fruits
            —Breads and cereals
        (2) Recognition and names of foods
          (a) For a good breakfast
          (b) For a good luncheon
          (c) For a good dinner or supper

THE FAMILY

Suggested Activities

V. The family (Cont'd)
  D. Family finances:
    12. See Unit on Clothing for suggested activities which can be used in teaching about clothing for the family.
    13. Discussion on providing adequate food for family.
    14. Plan well-balanced meals and make out shopping lists to provide these food supplies for a week or so. Figure out costs and discuss what portion of the family's income must be used for a *given* family income.
    15. Make a school store and practice buying groceries in the school room. Buy right kinds of foods to eat.
    16. Discussion on what to consider in buying food, such as storage facilities, cutting corners, buying foods in larger quantities, thrift in the use of foods, etc.
    17. Discussions on where food comes from, what are some of the contributing factors in price or cost of food, should we have a garden if possible, etc.
    18. Have homemaking teacher or food specialist talk to class on some of above subjects.
    19. Show some of the movies on foods, their source, preparation, etc., that are listed at the end of this Unit.
    20. Discussions about good table manners. Prepare a meal in homemaking room, and practice using good table manners.
    21. Social-dramas on table manners.
    22. Discussion on importance of family meals, pointing out that meal time should be a happy time, and a family occasion.
    23. Make scrap books about family meals showing pictures of family's enjoying meal time, pictures of well planned meals, etc.
    24. Make bulletin board using picturesque advertising posters, ads, etc.

THE FAMILY

Content Outline:

V. The family (Cont'd)
   D. Family Finances:
     5. Food for the family (cont'd)
       (3) Planned shopping lists
       (4) Prices and what makes food cost
         (a) Quantity
         (b) Quality
         (c) Transportation
         (d) Availability—seasonal foods, etc.
         (e) Competition
       (5) Storage facilities
         (a) Refrigeration
           —Refrigeration
           —Home freezer
         (b) Canning
     b. Conserving food
       (1) Extravagance and waste
       (2) Dangers of over-eating
       (3) Dangers of eating between meals
     c. Importance of family meals
       (1) Should be a happy occasion
       (2) Table manners
       (3) Whole family should eat together as much as possible. (Meal-time is family get together)
     6. Family Recreation
     a. Recreation in the home
       (1) Reading
         (a) Individual reading
           —Reading for pleasure
           —Reading for information
         (b) Family reading
           —Reading together for fun
           —Family study
       (2) Music
         (a) Record player
         (b) Television
         (c) Radio
         (d) Playing musical instrument
         (e) Singing

THE FAMILY

Suggested Activities:

V. The family (Cont'd)
  D. Family finances
    25. Take field trips to various food stores, canning factories, truck farms, dairy farms, poultry farms, bakeries, cheese factories and other food sources and processors.
    26. Discussion about types of recreation that a family can have in their home. Bring out each type of recreation listed in content outline.
    27. Discussion about family recreation being the responsibility of each member of the family. There must be family cooperation—give and take—in planning and participating in family recreation.
    28. Have students make a list of all kinds of games they can think of that they can play at home indoors and outdoors. Then have them play all of the games listed in the classroom so that they can learn how to play them. Teach correct rules of games, fair play, and good manners and attitudes in participation in any recreational activities.
    29. Have students make a class notebook on games including names of games and the correct rules of the games. Include pictures of family recreational activities.
    30. Discussion on handicrafts and hobbies in the family. Teach simple handicrafts in the classroom, and point out that many of the handicrafts the students learn in Manual Training and Occupational Therapy can be used for recreation in the home. They can help decorate their homes, and sometimes their hobbies can bring in supplementary incomes for their families. Include pictures of hobbies and handicrafts in class notebooks.
    31. Make a bulletin board display or table display of class members' hobbies Display things the students have made already in hobbies or craft classes.
    32. Discussion on using music as a recreational or relaxing activity. Teach students to listen to music on records, radio, etc., for enjoyment and relaxation. Give them practice in listening to different kinds of music—music that is stimulating, and other types that are relaxing.

THE FAMILY

Content Outline

V. The family: (Cont'd)
  D. Family finances:
    6. Family recreation (Cont'd)
      (3) Games—
        (a) Inside
        (b) Outside
      (4) Parties—
        (a) Sharing in planning and work
        (b) Responsibilities of each member of family to help make party successful
      (5) Handicrafts and hobbies
    b. Recreation away from home—
      (1) Picnics and excursions
      (2) Movies, plays, music
      (3) Dancing
      (4) Sports— (various types)
      (5) Amusement parks
      (6) Vacations
      (7) Roller skating
      (8) Swimming
      (9) Etc.

THE FAMILY

Suggested Activities

V. The family (Cont'd)
  D. Family finances
    33. Discussion on family singing, and the use of music to strengthen family ties.
    34. Discussion on proper use of television—watching right kinds of programs—not letting it interfere with other things that the family should do, etc.
    35. Discussion on reading for enjoyment—What to read—How to read for enjoyment and relaxation, etc.
    36. Discussion on how to plan a party and send invitations. Have students plan a party, and invite others to it. Teach co-operation and responsibility in planning the party and entertaining at the time of the party.
    37. Discussion on types of recreation the family can enjoy away from home. Bring in all types listed in content outline. Discuss planning picnics and excursions. Plan a picnic and have a class picnic having each member of the class take care of his part of the planning and his responsibilities for the picnic.
    38. Discussion on movies, plays, musical performance, etc. Discuss types that are good for families, those that are not, etc. Discuss movies that students have seen, and determine the desirability of a family seeing that kind of movie together.
    39. Teach various kinds of dances to the students and have them practice doing them in the class-room. Square dance, folk dances, fox trots, etc.
    40. Plan to attend some sports activities after discussing types of sports for the family to watch or participate in.
    41. Discuss and visit a nearby amusement park.
    42. Have class members plan family vacation in the class for different periods of time. Discuss them in the classroom.

THE FAMILY

Content Outline:

V. The family
    E. The family and the community:
        1. Respecting the rights of others in the community and elsewhere.
        2. Taking care of public property and respect for others' property.
        3. Obeying laws
            a. Federal
            b. State
            c. Local
            d. Traffic
            e. Licenses, permits, fees, etc.

THE FAMILY

Suggested Activities:

V. The family (Cont'd)

 E. The family and the community:

 1. Class discussions on obeying laws of federal, state, and local government, or government in the community. Point out that this is respecting the rights of others, and that these laws are for our own protection as well as for others.

 Discuss zoning laws, etc.

 2. Discussion on rights of others. Who has rights—why?, etc. Do we have a right to abuse the rights of others?, etc. Have socio-dramas on daily situations in which the rights of others are being abused.

 3. Discussion on care of personal property, and how this affects the community in which you live. What you do is not just your own business, because it affects the rights and property of others around you.

 Find pictures of personal property items.

 4. Discussion on care of public property in your community and all communities. Who pays expenses or maintenance, etc., of this property? What is public property?

 Find pictures of public property.

 5. Discussions on traffic laws—what are some of them? Why are they necessary, what is the punishment for breaking them, etc.? Take a field trip to a traffic court to observe traffic violations, and punishment for them.

 6. Discussion on licenses and permits that we must have to do and participate in various specific activities in own community and elsewhere.

 7. Discussions on getting along with neighbors in a community. Make a list of things that cause trouble between neighbors.

THE FAMILY

Content Outline:

V. The family
     F. The home:
          1. Choosing a place to live:
               a. Types or kinds of homes
               b. Prices for renting and owning homes of various types
          2. Things needed in furnishing a home:
               a. Furniture
               b. Floor coverings
               c. Kitchen utensils
               d. Dishes
               e. Silverware
               f. Cleaning implements
               g. Household appliances
               h. Drapes, curtains, pictures
               i. Bedding and linens
          3. Care of the home:
               a. Each member's responsibilities
               b. Safety in the home
               c. Routine maintenance
               d. Seasonal maintenance
               e. Other
               f. Cleaning

THE FAMILY

Suggested Activities:

V. The family
  F. The home:
    1. Discussions about kinds of homes in which a family can live, apartments, private homes, rent, own, etc. How much do they cost— What are costs involved in maintenances, etc. Discuss students own home—What kind—expense, etc.
    2. Field trip to see various types of homes, and talk to owner or real estate agent regarding costs, etc.
    3. Make a class note book including pictures of various types of homes and costs of each, etc.
    4. Have students make scrap books showing pictures of family members, and the things that must be provided in the home to make it a home that is successfully planned and equipped.
       Use catalogs and magazines to find pictures and prices of articles. Add all the prices together and discuss total cost, and how long it might take to acquire all of the provisions.
    5. Discuss maintenance and care of home, its furnishings, and other family belongings.
    6. Discussion on care of the home. Point out that this is the responsibility of each member of the family. Routines and habits can aid in proper care and maintenance of home.
    7. Discuss safe living in the home—repairing broken and damaged parts—frayed electrical wiring, eliminating poor cooking habits, medicine cabinets out of reach, and many other things that aid in healthful and safe living in the home.
    8. Show movies that are listed at the end of this Unit on safe living in the home.

THE FAMILY

Suggested Activities:

V. The family:
Suggested movies to be shown with the unit on The Family:
Parts A & B & C
Family responsibilities
Parents as providers
Children's responsibilities
The family unit
How to Raise a Boy—Du Pont Farm Film Foundation
Family Affair—Du Pont Farm Film Foundation
Friendship Begins at Home—ROA—Modern Talking Picture
Acts of Courtesy—ROA—Modern Talking Picture
It Takes All Kinds—Wisconsin State Board of Health
Control Your Emotions—ROA—Modern Talking Picture
Farewell to Childhood—Wisconsin State Board of Health
As Your Home Goes—Modern Talking Picture
Place Called Home—Princeton Film Center, Inc.
Fitness Is a Family Affair—Wisconsin State Board of Health
How Do You Know It's Love—Wisconsin State Board of Health
Morning With Jimmy—Association Films, Inc.
Part D
Family finances:
Yours to Keep—Modern Talking Picture
The Carpenter—United Brotherhood of Carpenters & Joiners of America
Family Life—Wisconsin State Board of Health
A Penny Saved—Credit Union National Association—Modern
The American Customer—Modern Talking Picture
So Much for so Little—Communicable Disease Center
Behind Each Sale—Modern Talking Picture
Peace of Mind—Sterling Movies, Inc.
Two Cheers for Charlie—Sterling Movies, Inc.
One out of Seven—Sterling Movies, Inc.

THE FAMILY

Suggested Activities:

V. The family:
  Suggested movies to be shown with the unit on The Family:
    Part D (Cont'd)
      Foods:
      Rainbow Harvest—Modern No. 110
      Treasure Island—Modern No. 78
      Meal Time Can Be a Happy Time—Wisconsin State Board of Health
      Citrus Contributions to Fresh for Health—Modern No. 1142
      Cows, Milk, and America—Modern No. 1182
      White Wonder—Modern
      American Harvest—General Motors, Inc.
      The Big Kitchen—Modern
      The Sun Goes North—Modern No. 161
      All Flesh Is Grass—American Cattlemen's Association
      Beef Maker—Modern No. 557
      A Nation's Meat—Swift and Company
      Green Giant's Magic—Modern Talking Picture—No. 514
      Potatoes Unlimited—Union Pacific Railroad—Dept. of Livestock & Agr.
      Fresh From the West—Union Pacific Railway
      Magic Cup—Modern No. 1008
      Crackers by the Billion—Modern No. 527
      Story of Oats and Oat Meal—Modern No. 562
      Bees and Honey—Free Film Guide—1959
      Chocolate Tree—Modern
      Beef and Carving—Free Film Guide
      In Partnership With Nature—Modern
        Recreation:
      Our Senior Citizens—New York Municipal—Broadcasting Company
      Holiday Afloat—National Association of Engine & Boat Manufacturers
      Woodland Manners—United States Forest Service
      What a Vacation—Ford Motor Company
      Fishing for Fun—General Motors Corporation
      This Is New York—Institute of Visual Communications, Inc.
      Day They Came to Tolliver Street—ROA

THE FAMILY

Suggested Activities:

V. The family:
Suggested movies to be shown with the unit on The Family:
Part E:
The family and the community:
Neighbors—Canadian Counselate General
Community Vector Control—Communicable Disease Center
Rat Killing—Communicable Disease Center
Survey of Refuse Disposal—Communicable Disease Center
Pure Water and Public Health—Modern
Part F:
The home—Care—Maintenance and safety of the home
Mrs. Hazard's House—National Society for Crippled Children & Adults
Doorway to Death—Aetna Life Affiliated Company
Your Safety First—General Motors Corporation
The Spray's the Thing—Du Pont and Company
Home Safe Home—Wisconsin State Board of Health
Let's Be Safe at Home—Wisconsin State Board of Health
Four Point Safety Home—Wisconsin State Board of Health
Make Your Home Safe—Wisconsin State Board of Health
Stop Fires—Save Jobs—Bureau of Communication Research, Inc.
Too Young to Burn—National Society for Crippled Children and Adults
How to Call the Fire Department—Bureau of Communication Research, Inc.
Crimes of Carelessness—Bureau of Communication Research, Inc.
Let's Play Safe—Wisconsin State Board of Health
Let's Think and Be Safe—General Motors—Wisconsin State Board of Health
Accidents Don't Just Happen—Communicable Disease Center
How to Have an Accident in the Home—National Society for Crippled Children & Adults
Homes for a Growing America—Modern
Home Safe Home—Wisconsin State Board of Health

MAKING FRIENDS

Objectives:

1. To determine what qualities make a good friend, where you can meet such people, and how to go about making their acquaintance.

Content Outline:

VI. Making friends:
    A. What is a good friend:
        1. Someone who has similar interests and abilities
        2. Someone who likes you as you are
        3. Someone who is not constantly changing
            a. Not moody
            b. Dependable and reliable
            c. Honest
            d. Cooperative
            e. Appreciative
            f. Sociable
            g. Courteous
            h. Has sense of humor
        4. A friendship that can survive differences
        5. A friendship with mutual respect
            a. Can appreciate others' point of view
        6. Someone who is neat and clean, who will not embarrass you in front of others
        7. A friend in need is a friend indeed
    B. Where can you find them:
        1. At Work
            a. Fellow workers often have some similar interests
            b. Often have same working hours
            c. Often have same financial status
            d. Often have same kinds of problems
        2. At play
            a. Recreational interests indicate same likes
            b. Often indicate relatively same financial status
        3. In church
            a. Wide choice with range in age, interests and abilities
            b. Is usually a fairly constant group
            c. More often than not of good character

MAKING FRIENDS

Suggested Activities:

VI. Making friends:
    A. What is a good friend:
        1. Class discussion on what makes a good friend:
           Bring out all points listed on the content outline. Point out that it is necessary for each member in the class to possess these characteristics if he is going to be a good friend to his friends also. We cannot expect this of others, even our friends, if we do not give it.
        2. Discussion on personality development:
        3. Discussion on good grooming and how it affects your art in making friends:
        4. Socio-dramas regarding friendship relationships:
    B. Where can you find them:
        1. Discussion regarding where and how we find and meet friends. Where are the best places to meet friends?
        2. Dramatize situations illustrating how people meet friends in these various situations.

MAKING FRIENDS

Content Outline:

VI. Making friends:
   C. How can you get acquainted:
      1. Working together:
         a. Daily contacts
         b. Eating lunch
         c. Riding to and from work
      2. Mutual acquaintances
         a. Introduced by friends
      3. Social contacts
         a. Parties
         b. Plant or office recreation and athletics
         c. Picnics, etc.

MAKING FRIENDS

Suggested Activities:

VI. Making friends:
    C. How can you get acquainted:
        1. Discuss various forms of introductions.
        2. Dramatize a number of situations on what to do and what not to to do in meeting friends.
        3. Discussion and practice on proper conversation between friends. Is it different between members of the opposite sex?

MOVIES:

My Hens and I—Mizrachi Women's Organization of America
It Takes All Kinds—Wisconsin State Board of Health
Acts of Courtesy—ROA—Modern Talking Pictures
Are You Popular—Wisconsin State Board of Health
Friendship Begins at Home—Modern
Control Your Emotions—Modern
As Your Homes Goes—Modern
Farewell to Childhood—Wisconsin State Board of Health
Personal Hygiene for Boys—Wisconsin State Board of Health
Ford People—Ford Motor Company
How to Raise a Boy—Du Pont and Farm Film Foundation
The Voice With a Smile Wins—Bell Telephone Company
Thanks for Listening—Bell Telephone Company

MONEY

Objectives:

1. To teach students to recognize coins and bills of our money system.
2. To help students learn the value of our money
3. To teach students to count money and to make change.
4. To teach students to write money values and how to figure these values in every day living situations.
5. To give students an understanding of approximately how much money they will be making, what will be deducted from their pay checks, and for what will they have to spend the remainder of their checks.
6. Help students understand how to budget their money for these things.

Content Outline:

VII. Money:
- A. Recognition of money:
  1. Penny
  2. Nickel
  3. Dime
  4. Quarter
  5. Half-dollar
  6. Dollar bill
  7. Five dollar bill
  8. Ten dollar bill
  9. Twenty dollar bill
- B. Realization of value of coins and bills:
  1. How much is a penny?
  2. How much is a nickel?
  3. How much is a dime?
  4. How much is a quarter?
  5. How much is a half-dollar?
  6. How much is a dollar?
  7. How many of the various coins does it take to make other coins?

MONEY

Suggested Activities:

VII. Money:
   A. Recognition of money:
   &
   B. Realization of value of coins and bills.
   1. Have class discussions and exercises teaching the recognition of all the various coins of our money system.
   Use real money in teaching the recognition of money to eliminate confusion of transferring from toy money to real money.
   2. Make illustrative charts out of masonite boards using the various coins, and the various combinations of coins contained in larger coins.
   3. Use real coins to let pupils handle them and learn to associate the value of the coin with the coin itself.
   4. Give written arithmetic problems for seat work to let pupils have practise and experience in thinking about and handling money.
   5. Give pupils real money to use in the classroom to form various combinations of coins which represent the same values as other coins.
   6. Make cross word puzzle about coins and their values.
   7. Play games teaching the recognition and values of all the various coins.

MONEY

Content Outline:

VII. Money:
    C. How do we count money?
        1. Count by pennies (1's)
        2. Count by nickels (5's)
        3. Count by dimes (10's)
        4. Count by quarters (25's)
        5. Count by half-dollars (50's)
        6. Count by dollars (1.00's)
        7. Count coins by switching from one coin to another from any point or number.
        8. Make change by counting from cost of article purchased to amount of money given by customer.

MONEY

Suggested Activities:

VII. Money:
  C. How do we count money?
  1. Class discussions about how to count money.
  2. Teach class to count by all the various coins by letting them count money to one another.
  3. Teach students to count by 1's; 5's; 10's; 25's; 50's; and all other counting combinations used in the counting of money by letting them count the coins to one another.
  4. Have a classroom store, and let students play store by buying and selling articles, paying for them and making change for them, to provide an exciting and interesting learning experience in handling money.
  5. Play games that involve handling and counting money, and making change so that students have a learning experience but enjoy the activity.
     a. Make color charts on bulletin board or black board with amounts of money written in squares on the chart. Count by 5's; 10's; 25's; etc. Shoot guns with rubber darts and have cashier pay the student, who shoots the gun, whatever amount of money the dart lands on. Make change to get the right amount of money. The one who has most money after each has had a turn is the winner, gets to be the cashier next time.
     b. Play musical chairs, but do the following instead of taking out another chair each time: Have a can or jar with teacher-made chips containing amounts of money, which the student who has been left without a chair, must pay the student who got his chair. Give each child a certain (equal) amount of money at the beginning. The one who has the most money at the end of the game is the winner.
     c. Make up various other games involving the use of money.
  6. Take a shopping field trip, and a field trip to a restaurant to order a meal to give practical experiences in the use of money and making change.

MONEY

Content Outline:

VII. Money:
    D. How do we write the values of money?
        1. What is the decimal? Use to separate dollars from cents
        2. Teach number position—1's place; 10's place; 100's place; 1,000's place; 10,000's place and 100,000's place, etc.
        3. Write the values of money—from .01 to .10
        4. Write the values of money—from .10 to 1.00
        5. Write the values of money—1.00 to 10.00
        6. Write the values of money—10.00 to 100.00
        7. Write the values of money—100.00 to 1,000.00, etc.
        8. Correct number position for adding and subtracting money

MONEY

Suggested Activities:

VII. Money:
  D. How do we write the values of money:
  1. Class discussions about the use of the decimal point pointing out that it is used to separate the dollars from the cents. Give illustrations on blackboard.
  2. Class discussions regarding number positions (the 1's place, 10's place, 100's place, etc.).
  3. Give class illustrations of the correct ways to write money when using the decimal point. Illustrate number positions and why we must write the numbers in the correct places when adding, subtracting, etc.
  4. Class drills in writing various amounts of money correctly.
  5. Teacher read various amounts of money, and let pupils write them in correct position for adding and subtracting.
  6. Written problem and exercises in problem solving, using every day practical situations involving the use of money.
  7. Make charts on tag board with felt point pens about every day situations involving the use of money in written form such as pay checks and statements with money values, etc.

MONEY

Content Outline:

VII. Money:
    E. Budgeting money:
        1. Approximately how much are we going to make? (Gross salary)
        2. Approximately what will be taken from our checks before we receive them? (Deductions)
            a. Social Security
            b. Federal Income Taxes
            c. Hospitalization Insurances
            d. Pensions
            e. Miscellaneous
        3. Approximately what will we have left? (Net salary)
        4. For what will we have to spend our net salary?
            a. Shelter
            b. Food
            c. Transportation
            d. Clothing
            e. Additional taxes—other than those deducted from pay check
            f. Utility bills (Misc.)
            g. Extra insurances—other than those deducted from pay check
            h. Recreation
            i. Savings
            j. Miscellaneous
        5. How much can we spend out of our salary for each of the above?

MONEY

Suggested Activities:

VII. Money:
- E. Budgeting money:
  1. Class discussions regarding approximately what would constitute an average salary for pupils getting unskilled jobs.
  2. Vocabulary study on words such as: Gross salary; net salary; deductions; social security; income taxes, etc.
  3. Class discussions pointing out the deductions that will probably be taken out of the gross salary and for what will they be used.
  4. Discussion about social security and the need for it. How it will be used, etc.
  5. Discussions about pensions—What they are for—Are they always part of the work plan—etc.
  6. Discussions about income taxes—Why must we pay them? Do we get any benefits from this money? Is this one of our responsibilities? How is this money used, etc.
  7. Review on hospitalization and medical insurances.
  8. Make large poster chart of a pay check with work statement attached listing gross salary, deductions, net salary, etc.
  9. Obtain samples of work statements of various types from surrounding industries and discuss them with the class.
  10. Discussions pertaining to what the pupils will have to spend the rest of their pay check for. Work out weekly and monthly budgets dividing their pay check into approximate amounts needed for shelter, food, transportation, clothing, insurances, recreation, savings, and miscellaneous expenses.
  11. Teacher can bring his own bills, bank statements, etc., each month and have pupils help pay them so they can have the experience of paying bills, balancing the check stubs with the bank statement, etc.
  12. Teacher can bring his own income taxes to school each year, and have students help to fill them out and send them to the proper place. This will give the students practical experiences doing the things discussed.

MONEY

Suggested Activities:

VII. Money:
    MOVIES:
    A Penny Saved—Modern—Credit Union National Association
    Family Life—Wisconsin State Board of Health
    The American Customer—Modern
    Production—Modern—Ford Motor Company
    Back of Every Promise—Continental Illinois Bank & Trust Company
    So Much for so Little—Communicable Disease Center
    Behind Each Sale—Modern
    The Littlest Giant—Modern
    Peace of Mind—Sterling Movies, Inc.
    One Out of Seven—Sterling Movies, Inc.
    Equation for Progress—Ford Motor Company
    'Til Debt Do Us Part—Modern
    Working Dollars—Modern

CLOTHING

Objectives:

1. To develop an understanding of clothing as to what is needed, where to obtain it and how to take care of it.

Content Outline:

VIII. Clothing:
    A. Needs:
        1. What is my size?
          a. Different articles
        2. Do I have enough clothes?
          a. Minimum essentials
        3. What do I need for different occasions
          a. Work
          b. Dress
          c. Leisure
          d. Seasons
          e. Weather
        4. Do I keep my clothes clean and repaired?
          a. Wash and use spot remover
          b. Pressed—use of iron
          c. Mended
          d. Shoes polished
    B. Purchases:
        1. Where can I buy what I need?
          a. Clothing Store
          b. Department Store
        2. What must I know?
          a. What sells the things I want
          b. Location and how to get there
          c. Size, color, materials for purpose and price
          d. Ride the elevator and escalator
          e. Finding the proper department
          f. Do I take the first article
          g. Should I wear it home
          h. Is the article worth the price
          i. Can I return it
          j. Should I wear it first

CLOTHING

Suggested Activities:

VIII. Clothing:
  A. Needs:
    1. Discussion on how sizes are measured for different articles of clothing. What size do you wear?
    2. Use student as model and take his measurements for complete wardrobe. Have each one determine his own sizes for different articles.
    3. Look up various articles of clothing in newspaper advertising and mail order catalogs—pick out sizes and check the costs.
    4. View visual materials and discuss how much clothing is necessary as the minimum essentials.
    5. Ask the question, "Do you have enough of each?" Compile a list of all the articles of clothing necessary for the various activities of an individual.
    6. Demonstrate how clothing can become dirty and damaged. Discuss what can be done about it.
    7. Make use of both washing and spot remover and display the results. Discuss the importance of following directions and the dangers of each method.
    8. Discuss the relative cost of maintenance and replacement. Have class participate in campaign on own clothing with mending, sewing on buttons and pressing in class.
    9. Conduct "before and after" demonstration on shining a pair of shoes. Discuss various kinds of polish and how to treat leather.
  B. Purchases:
    1. Review on the clothing needs of the individual for various occasions.
    2. Discussion on various kinds of stores that handle the clothing the individual needs. How do they differ?
    3. Demonstrate the proper way to purchase articles of clothing. Set up clothing store in school and have the classes visit and order various articles of clothing.
    4. Make up order for complete clothing wardrobe from mail order catalog or newspaper putting the price of article down.
    5. Plan and visit clothing stores in the nearby communities. Follow-up discussion to answer questions on problems that arose.

CLOTHING

Content Outline:

VIII. Clothing:
    C. Cleaning and maintenance:
        1. What can be washed and what has to be dry cleaned?
          a. Individual garments
        2. Can I wash my own clothes?
          a. Proper materials and procedure
          b. Use of washerettes or self-service laundry
        3. Laundry and dry cleaners:
          a. What are they
          b. Where are they located
          c. How do they operate
        4. What must I know?
          a. How much to send
          b. Is it picked up and delivered
          c. How long does it take
          d. What to do if something is lost
          e. What to send—mark each piece
          f. Cost—per article
          g. Can I afford all or part of it

CLOTHING

Suggested Activities:

VIII. Clothing:
  C. Cleaning and maintenance:
    1. Discussion on which garments can be washed and which have to be dry-cleaned. Provide examples of each.
    Discuss and show various kinds of materials used in making clothing.
    2. Compare costs of cleaning and laundering. How often should garments be cleaned or washed? What factors affect this frequency?
    3. Discussion on proper materials and procedure for washing own clothes. Each member bring garment for demonstration. Use hand wash, washing machine and automatic washer.
    4. Demonstration on washing own clothes comparing cost and advantages of each method.
    5. Discussion on use of self-service laundries. Display visual materials and visit such an establishment.
    6. Discussion on regular laundries and how they operate. Emphasize what has to be done to prepare clothes. Be sure to keep record.
    7. Compare cost of self-laundering and regular laundering. Discounts for bringing in and picking up. Plan and visit regular laundry in nearby community.—Can use institution facility.
    8. Review which garments have to be dry cleaned. Discussion on where to take them (use classified section of phone book). Compare costs with laundering.
    9. Plan and visit to dry cleaning plant in nearby community. View and discuss any visual materials that are available.

CLOTHING

Suggested Activities:

VIII. Clothing:
MOVIES:
Border Weave—Wool Bureau, Inc.
Uncle Henry Saves the Play—Modern
Co-op Wool From Fleece to Fabric—Farm Credit Banks
Cotton—Nature's Wonder Film—National Cotton Council of America
Facts About Fabrics—Du Pont de Nemours and Company, Inc.
Romance of Silk—Japan Tourist Association
Two-Hour Miracle—Du Pont

RECREATION

Objectives:

1. To introduce and interest the youth in a variety of recreation activities in which he can participate at his own level during his leisure time.
2. To help student become acquainted with opportunities and locations for individual or group recreation that are available in the community throughout the year (participant or spectator).
3. To demonstrate and explain to the student a variety of activities that can be utilized for leisure time in the home situation.

Content Outline:

IX. Recreation and use of leisure time:
   A. Recreation outside the home:
      1. Y.M.C.A. & Y.W.C.A.
         a. Club activities
            (1) Variety of subjects
            (2) Way of making friends
         b. Gymnasium
            (1) Physical conditioning
            (2) Swimming
         c. Games
            (1) Cards
            (2) Checkers
            (3) Table Tennis
         d. Reading room
            (1) Newspapers
            (2) Magazines
            (3) Comics
         e. Craft activities
            (1) Simple with little cost
            (2) Instruction available
         f. Dancing
            (1) Social
            (2) Square and Folk
         g. Camping
            (1) Group
      2. Public Library
         a. Books
            (1) How to draw out
         b. Records
            (1) Listening
         c. Magazines and newspapers
            (1) Use in reading room
            (2) Draw out

RECREATION

Suggested Activities:

IX. Recreation and use of leisure time:
  A. Recreation outside the home:
  1. Visit various community organizations to see what is available and discuss types of activities to suit different people.
  2. Have reading table in classroom which has newspapers, etc., on it and give students time to read and discuss them.
  3. Discuss what each student feels he would like to do with his leisure time and where these activities might be carried on.
  4. Provide game table in the room with various card games, etc., on it so student can learn and practice them.
  5. Do various craft activities and have each student keep a notebook as to how the activities are carried out so it can be used for future reference.
  6. Teach some common steps in ballroom dancing explaining that further instruction and practice can be obtained if necessary. Review square dancing and discuss where it is being held.
  7. Visit public libraries and point out differences between main and branches. Discuss library conduct and make-out application for a card. Practice drawing out books.
  8. Visit large public park which has zoo, play areas, etc., and point out different activities and how they can be carried on. Survey the cost in different activities.
  9. Get a brochure from a nearby museum and discuss the various activities carried on at the museum. Plan and visit the museum explaining displays and other activities.
  10. Take field trips to view baseball games, basketball games, etc., when the opportunity presents itself.
  11. Plan picnics, and give students opportunity to use public parks in the community.
  12. Teach pupils to play various card games, and play with them in the classroom.

RECREATION

Content Outline:

IX. Recreation and use of leisure time:
   A. Recreation outside the home: (Cont'd)
      3. Public Parks
         a. Zoo
            (1) Visiting the animals
            (2) Taking a walk
            (3) Taking pictures
         b. Play areas
            (1) Ball
            (2) Horseshoe
            (3) Skating
            (4) Swimming
            (5) Boat rides
            (6) Picnics
         c. Spectator
            (1) Movies
            (2) Band concerts
            (3) Ball games
            (4) Racing
            (5) Fairs
            (6) Flower Exhibits
            (7) Horse show
         d. Winter activities
            (1) Ice skating
            (2) Tobogganing
            (3) Skiing
      4. Museum
         a. Exhibits
            (1) Variety of subjects
            (2) No cost
            (3) Guides available
         b. Lectures
            (1) Travel and adventure
            (2) Homemaking
         c. Clubs
            (1) Hobby
            (2) Sporting

RECREATION

Content Outline:

IX. Recreation and use of leisure time:
  A. Recreation outside the home:
    5. Movies and the Theater
      a. Movies
        (1) Choice of pictures
        (2) Cost (price change)
      b. Theater
        (1) How it differs from movies
        (2) More expensive
    6. Sports:
      a. Baseball
        (1) School
        (2) League teams
        (3) Softball
        (4) Woman's games
      b. Football
        (1) School
        (2) Amateur
        (3) Professional
      c. Auto racing
        (1) Midget
        (2) Stock car
        (3) Big car
      d. Horse racing
        (1) Fairs (sulky)
        (2) Jockey
      e. Boxing and wrestling
        (1) School
        (2) Amateur
        (3) Community center
        (4) Public hall
      f. Bowling
        (1) Individual
        (2) League
      g. Golf and tennis
        (1) Public facilities
      h. Industrial sports
        (1) Conjunction with work

RECREATION

Content Outline:

IX. Recreation and use of leisure time:
   A. Recreation outside the home:
      7. Miscellaneous Activities
         a. Church
            (1) Young people's groups
         b. Evening schools
            (1) Social centers
            (2) Vocational centers
         c. Hunting and fishing
            (1) Rural areas
            (2) Seasons and necessity for license
         d. Bicycle riding
            (1) Rural and urban areas
         e. Sight seeing
            (1) Bus
            (2) Streetcar
         f. Amusement parks
            (1) Variety of activities

RECREATION

Content Outline:

IX. Recreation and use of leisure time:
  B. Recreation in or near the Home:
    1. Hobbies:
      a. Modeling
        (1) All types (clay, wood, airplane)
      b. Collecting
        (1) Stamps
        (2) Coins
        (3) Others
      c. Scrap books
        (1) May be part of collecting
      d. Craftwork
        (1) Instruction
        (2) Practice
      e. Aquarium-Terrarium
        (1) Various kinds of fish
      f. Simple photography
        (1) Develop interest in taking pictures
      g. Simple musical instruments
        (1) Mouth organ
      h. Care of pets
        (1) Dog or cat
        (2) Farm animals
        (3) Rabbit
    2. Active activities
      a. Gardening
        (1) Flowers, shrubs, vegetable
      b. Washing the car
        (1) May provide extra income
      c. Lawn games
        (1) Croquet
        (2) Horse shoe
      d. Ice skating
        (1) Park or playground
      e. Ball game
        (1) Playground
        (2) Empty lot

RECREATION

Suggested Activities:

IX. Recreation and use of leisure time:
    B. Recreation in or near the home:
        See suggested activities in the unit on The Family (Part D):

RECREATION

Content Outline:

IX. Recreation and use of leisure time:
  B. Recreation in or near the home:
    2. Passive Activities: (Cont'd)
      d. Reading
        (1) Books
        (2) Newspapers
        (3) Magazines
        (4) Comics
      e. Looking at pictures
        (1) Part of reading
      f. Letter writing
        (1) Be able to write a letter
      g. General conversation
        (1) What to talk about
        (2) What not to talk about
      h. Art activities
        (1) Use of crayons
        (2) Use of water colors
        (3) Color books
    3. Games:
      a. Checkers
        (1) Skill with practice
      b. Chess
        (1) More difficult
      c. Card playing
        (1) Variety of games
      d. Dominoes
        (1) Can be taught in school
      e. Dice games
        (1) Do not have to be gambling
      f. Puzzles
        (1) Non-language
    4. Personal Business
      a. Cleaning of the room
        (1) Putting things in their places
      b. Personal grooming
        (1) Bathing (washing of hair)
        (2) Shaving
        (3) Teeth
        (4) Keeping clothes clean and repaired
        (5) Use of cosmetics

RECREATION

Suggested Activities:

IX. Recreation and use of leisure time:
   MOVIES:
   Holiday Afloat—National Association of Engine and Boat Manufacturers
   What a Vacation—Ford Motor Company
   Woodland Manners—United States Forest Service
   Fishing for Fun—General Motors Corp.
   This Is New York—Institute of Visual Communications, Inc.
   Day They Came to Tolliver Street—ROA, Inc.
   Our Senior Citizens—New York Municipal Broadcasting Company
   Canyon Country—Ford Motor Company
   Dearborn Holiday—Ford Motor Company
   Highway by the Sea—Ford Motor Company
   Yellowstone—Ford Motor Company
   Skyline New York—Institute of Visual Communications, Inc.
   West to the Tetons—Ford Motor Company
   Let's Take a Trip—Modern
   Flight to California—Institute of Visual Communications, Inc.
   Southern Hilanders—Ford Motor Company
   The Dynamic Southeast—Association Films or United World Free Film Service
   Alaska Holiday—Allis Chalmers Manufacturing Company (Allis-Chalmers)
   California Zephyr—Western Pacific Railroad
   Fascination Florida Keys—Florida Development Commission
   Greatest Show on Water—Kiekhæfer, Corp.
   Valley of Light—Ford Motor Company
   Ozark Interlude—Missouri Division of Resources & Development
   California—A World in a Week
   Mid-West Holiday—Ideal Pictures, Inc.
   America in Pictures—
   Boston—City of Yesterday and Tomorrow—Boston Convention & Visitor's Bureau
   Camping Together—Good Neighbor Commission of Texas
   Frying Pan and the Fire—United States Forest Service
   Glacier National Park—Modern
   Wyoming Adventure—Ford Motor Company
   White Thunder—Ford Motor Company

SAFETY

Objectives:

1. To develop better judgment in situations presenting danger in individual or group experiences.
2. To encourage students to practice practical safety habits in every day situations in the home and community.
3. To teach recognition of safety signs and signals which will enable the students to protect themselves and live more safely in the community.
4. To learn the laws and rules for traffic, pedestrians, and people on bicycles, which will help them and people around them live more safely in the community.
5. To develop appreciation for laws that protect society and help the students understand why it is necessary for all to obey laws and rules that are designed to provide safety for all.
6. To influence attitudes and behavior that are conducive to safe living in the home and the community and that will contribute cooperation with agencies and departments aiding safety in the community.

Content Outline:

X. Safety:
    A. Safety in the home:
        1. Hazards causing wounds:
            a. Pointed objects
            b. Sharp edges—tin, glass, blades
            c. Heavy objects falling
        2. Hazards causing falls:
            a. Toys out of place
            b. Climbing
            c. Slippery surfaces
            d. Unprotected windows
            e. Throw rugs without proper protection from sliding
            f. Untidy stairways

SAFETY

Suggested Activities:

X. Safety:
  A. Safety in the home:
   1. Class discussions about hazards in the home that cause wounds such as pointed objects, sharp edges, heavy objects, etc. What are some of these objects? What can we do to avoid accidents caused by them? etc.
   2. Have class make lists of as many objects as they can think of which can cause wounds in the home.
   3. Ask students to tell about incidents in their own homes which caused accidents by some of the above mentioned objects.
   4. Have socio-dramas illustrating accidents of this type to the class.
   5. Display posters illustrating accidents in the home. Discuss these posters. Let members of the class explain what is happening.
   6. Class discussions on hazards causing burns. How can they be prevented? What should be done when they happen? Where can one obtain help, etc.?
   7. Show movies on First Aid followed by discussions and demonstrations. These movies on First Aid should include all kinds of accidents and the proper care to be given for various kinds of injuries.
   8. Discussions on hazards of electrical appliances and the importance of using them properly and keeping them properly repaired.
   9. Class discussions and demonstrations illustrating the dangers of keeping poisonous materials around where they can be accidentally used. Where should these articles be kept and why?

SAFETY

Content Outline:

X. Safety:
  A. Safety in the home:
    3. Hazards causing burns, scalds:
      a. Matches
      b. Kitchen not a place to play in
        (1) Stoves
        (2) Boiling or hot water
        (3) Chemicals
        (4) Hot foods cooking in hot pots and pans
      c. Misplaced pot handles
      d. Cleaning fluids
      e. Untested bath water
      f. Explosives
    4. Electrical hazards:
      a. Outlets
      b. Broken equipment
      c. Wet hands
      d. Electric fans and appliances
      e. Christmas tree and party decorations
      f. Electric toys
    5. Hazards from poisons:
      a. Medicines
      b. Cleaning fluids

SAFETY

Suggested Activities

X. Safety:
  A. Safety in the home:
    10. Have a doctor or nurse talk to the class about common accidents in the home and how they should be treated.
    11. Show film strips about safety in the home.
    12. Make bulletin board displays illustrating the common mistakes that cost us many lives and dollars each year.
    13. Make class notebooks regarding home accidents and how they can be avoided. Include pictures, safety rules, common dangers in the home, and all things discussed in the class.
    14. Demonstrate many of the things discussed in this unit on work by having a classroom television program about safety. Have the students make up the program and prepare the television stage in the classroom, etc.

SAFETY

Content Outline:

X. Safety:
  B. Safety in the community:
    1. Safety precautions away from the home:
      a. Public places
        (1) Playgrounds
        (2) Parks
        (3) Swimming pools
        (4) Street safety
          (a) Proper crossings
          (b) Obedience to signals
      b. Large gatherings
        (1) Parades
        (2) Carnivals—fairs
        (3) Movies—theaters
        (4) Dances
        (5) Holiday shopping
      c. Travel safety
        (1) Manners while waiting for a vehicle
        (2) Manners on boarding a vehicle
        (3) Manners in a vehicle
        (4) Manners on leaving a vehicle
        (5) Obeying traffic laws
        (6) Obeying pedestrian laws
      d. Safety signs
        (1) Recognize and read
        (2) Note where seen
      e. Seasonal safety
        (1) Winter safety
        (2) Summer safety
        (3) Spring safety
        (4) Fall safety

SAFETY

Suggested Activities:

X. Safety:
  B. Safety in the community:
    1. Class discussions on safety in public places such as playgrounds, parks, swimming pools, etc. Emphasize use of manners in these places, and that common courtesy prevents many accidents.
    2. Have socio-dramas in the class illustrating situations that cause accidents in these places. After each socio-drama, illustrate how these situations could have been prevented.
    3. Have artists of the classroom draw pictures or have all the students find pictures illustrating situations of these types of accidents, and then have them discuss each picture and point out what is happening, and what could have prevented this situation.
    4. Show movies about accidents and safety in public places.
    5. Display safety posters which can be obtained from your nearest safety council. Make bulletin boards about the subject of safety in the various areas mentioned in the content outline.
    6. Class discussions on safety in large crowds or gatherings such as parades, carnivals, fairs, movies, theaters, dances, etc.
    7. Have class members make lists of as many accidents as they can think of that could happen in such situations.
    8. Class discussions pertaining to manners to use while riding on any type of vehicle used in public transportation. How will the use of these manners keep us from having more accidents?
    9. Class discussions about traffic laws and pedestrian rules and regulations. Why do we have such laws? What happens when we disobey them? etc.
    10. Take field trips and use various types of public transportation. Observe the manners used by the people on the vehicles. Point out dangers and reasons for practising the manners that were previously discussed.
    11. Obtain posters and traffic signs from the State Motor Vehicle Department. Make such signs if they cannot be obtained from the State Department. Use these signs in the classroom to teach the students to recognize them and follow the rules regarding them. Use these signs to teach safety vocabulary.
    12. Have vocabulary drills to teach the safety vocabulary.

SAFETY

Content Outline:

X. Safety:
    B. Safety in the community:
        2. Cooperation with departments aiding safety:
            a. Police Department
                (1) Know personal history
                (2) Know and observe traffic rules
                (3) Know and observe pedestrian rules
                (4) Report hazards and accidents
            b. Fire Department
                (1) Know when and how to call an alarm
                (2) Know various duties and interests of the fire department
                (3) Know and observe the fire prevention rules

SAFETY

Suggested Activities:

X. Safety:
B. Safety in the community:
13. Class discussions pertaining to seasonal safety. Point out the necessity for wearing proper clothing for each season of the year. Discuss such things as safety on ice and snow in the winter, safety pertaining to the thawing of ice in the spring, the changing of weather conditions in spring and fall, etc. Point out the dangers of too much sun in the summer and other hazards of the seasons.
14. Class discussions about police and fire departments and how they help us. When do we use them? How do we get them when we need them?
15. Have a policeman and a fireman come to the class and talk to the class members.
16. Take field trips to the police department and to the fire department pointing out how these departments are used to provide safety for all citizens even those who are the law-breakers. Discuss how each citizen can cooperate and help these departments for the safety and protection of all.
17. Practise calling the police and fire departments by phone in the classroom. Teachers can obtain telephone sets called tele-trainers from their local Bell Telephone Companies.
18. Show movies from the list of movies on the subject of Safety which are listed at the end of this unit.

SAFETY

Suggested Activities:

X. Safety:
  MOVIES:
  Home Safe Home—Wisconsin State Board of Health
  Let's Be Safe at Home—Wisconsin State Board of Health
  Mrs. Hazard's House—National Society for Crippled Children
  Doorway to Death—Aetna Life Affiliated Company
  Your Safety First—General Motors Corp. (First)
  The Spray's the Thing—Du Pont, and Company
  Four Point Safety Home—Wisconsin State Board of Health
  Make Your Home Safe—Wisconsin State Board of Health
  Stop Fires—Safe—Jobs—Bureau of Communication Research
  Too Young to Burn—National Society for Crippled Children and Adults
  How to Call the Fire Department—Bureau of Communication Research, Inc.
  Crimes of Carelessness—Bureau of Communication Research, Inc.
  Let's Play Safe—Wisconsin State Board of Health
  Let's Think and Be Safe—General Motors—Wisconsin State Board of Health
  Accidents Don't Just Happen—Communicable Disease Center
  How to Have an Accident in the Home—National Society for Crippled Children and Adults
  When You Are a Pedestrian—Employers Mutuals of Wausau
  All of a Sudden—Modern
  Case of Officer Hallibrand—Modern
  And Then There Were Four—Modern
  How to Fight Fire in the Kitchen—Bureau of Communication Research, Inc.
  First Aid I—American Red Cross
  First Aid II—American Red Cross
  Hook—Line and Safety—Aetna Life Affiliated Companies

5

FILM TITLES AND SOURCES OF MOVIES AND MATERIALS LISTED IN THIS CURRICULUM

A

About Faces .... United States Public Health Services
Accidents Don't Just Happen .... Communicable Disease Center
Acts of Courtesy .... ROA ... or Modern Talking Pictures, Inc.
Adventures in Dairyland .... Modern Talking Pictures, Inc. No. 1153
Alaska Holiday .... Allis-Chalmers Manufacturing Co.
All Flesh Is Grass .... American Cattlemen's Association
All of a Sudden .... Modern Talking Pictures, Inc.
As Your Home Goes .... Modern Talking Pictures, Inc.
America in Pictures ....
American Customer, The .... Modern Talking Pictures, Inc.
American Harvest .... General Motors
A Nation's Meat .... Swift and Company
And Then There Were Four .... Modern Talking Pictures, Inc.
Another Light .... Communicable Disease Center
Any Boy U.S.A. .... National W.C.T.U. ... Evanston, Illinois
A Penny Saved .... Credit Union National Association
                                      Also ... Modern Talking Pictures, Inc.
Are You Popular .... Wisconsin State Board of Health
As Your Home Goes .... Modern Talking Pictures, Inc.

B

Back of Every Promise .... Continental Illinois National Bank and
                                      Trust Company
Beef and Carving .... Modern Talking Pictures, Inc.
Beef Maker .... Modern Talking Pictures, Inc. No. 557
Bees and Honey .... Farm Film Foundation
Big Kitchen, The .... Modern Talking Pictures, Inc.
Border Weave .... Wool Bureau, Inc.
Boston—City of Yesterday and Tomorrow Boston Convention & Visitor's Bureau
Brain Is the Reason, The .... National W.C.T.U. ... Evanston, Illinois

C

California—A World in a Week .... Union Pacific Railroad
California Zephyr .... Western Pacific Railroad
Camping Together .... Good Neighbor Commission of Texas
Canyon Country .... Ford Motor Co.
Carpenter, The .... United Brotherhood of Carpenters and
                                      Joiners of America

152

Case of Officer Hallibrand .... Modern Talking Pictures, Inc.
Chance of a Life Time, The .... National W.C.T.U. ... Evanston, Illinois
Chocolate Tree .... Modern Talking Pictures, Inc.
Choice Is Yours, The .... National W.C.T.U. ... Evanston, Illinois
Circulation of the Blood .... American Heart Association
Citrus Contributions to Fresh for Health Modern Talking Pictures, Inc. No. 1142
Clean Look, The .... Modern Talking Pictures, Inc. No. 150
Color of Health .... American Baker's Association
Common Cold .... Wisconsin State Board of Health
Community Vector Control .... Community Disease Center
Confessions of a Cold .... Wisconsin State Board of Health
Control Your Emotions .... Modern Talking Pictures, Inc.
Coop Wool From Fleece to Fabric .... Farm Credit Districts
Cotton—Nature's Wonder Fiber .... National Cotton Council of America
Cows, Milk, and America .... Modern Talking Pictures, Inc. No. 1182
Crackers by the Billion .... Modern Talking Pictures, Inc. No. 527
Crimes of Carelessness .... Bureau of Communication Research, Inc.

D

Day They Came to Tolliver Street ..... ROA, Inc.
Dearborn Holiday .... Ford Motor Co.
Defense Against Invasion .... Wisconsin State Board of Health
Denny's Dental Date .... Wisconsin State Board of Health
Dollars and Sense .... National W.C.T.U. ... Evanston, Illinois
Doorway to Death .... Aetna Life Affiliated Company
Dynamic Southeast, The .... Association Films, or ... United World
Free Film Service

E

Engineering Your Health .... Communicable Disease Center
Equation for Progress .... Ford Motor Co.
Even for One .... Sterling Movies U.S.A., Inc.

F

Fact or Fancy .... National W.C.T.U. ... Evanston, Illinois
Facts About Fabrics .... Du Pont de Nemours and Co., Inc.
Faith in Boys .... General Motors
Family Affair .... Du Pont de Nemours and Co., Inc.
Family Life .... Wisconsin State Board of Health
Farewell to Childhood .... Wisconsin State Board of Health
Fascination Florida Keys .... Florida Development Commission
50,000 Lives .... Association Films Inc.
First Aid I .... American Red Cross
First Aid II .... American Red Cross
Fishing for Fun .... General Motors Corp.
Fitness Is a Family Affair .... Wisconsin State Board of Health
Flight to California .... Institute of Visual Communications, Inc.
Fly Control Through Basic Sanitation .. Communicable Disease Center

K

King Who Came to Breakfast, The .... Association Films, Inc.
Kitty Cleans Up .... Wisconsin State Board of Health

L

Lease on Life .... Wisconsin State Board of Health
Let's Be Safe at Home .... Wisconsin State Board of Health
Let's Have Fewer Colds .... Wisconsin State Board of Health
Let's Play Safe .... Wisconsin State Board of Health
Let's Take a Trip .... Modern Talking Pictures, Inc.
Let's Think and Be Safe .... General Motors Corporation
Life of a Healthy Child .... Wisconsin State Board of Health
Losing to Win .... Modern Talking Pictures, Inc. No. 1120

M

Magic Cup .... Modern Talking Pictures, Inc.
Magic of Vision .... Better Vision Institute
Make Your Home Safe .... Wisconsin State Board of Health
Man on the Land .... United World Free Film Service . . . also
                                       American Petroleum Institute
Mealtime Can Be a Happy Time .... Wisconsin State Board of Health
Measure of a Man .... Modern Talking Pictures, Inc. No. 788
Mid-West Holiday .... Ideal Pictures
Milk Parade .... Wisconsin State Board of Health
Modern Guide to Health .... Wisconsin State Board of Health
Molly Grows Up .... Wisconsin State Board of Health
Morning With Jimmy .... Association Films, Inc.
Mr. Finley's Feelings .... Metropolitan Life Insurance Company
Mrs. Hazard's House .... National Society for Crippled Children

O

O'Mara's Chain Miracle .... General Motors Corporation
One Out of Seven .... Sterling Movies, Inc.
Our Senior Citizens .... New York Municipal Broadcasting
                                       Company
Ozark Interlude .... Missouri Division of Resources and
                                       Development

P

Peace of Mind .... Sterling Movies, Inc.
Personal Hygiene for Boys .... Wisconsin State Board of Health
Place Called Home .... Princeton Film Center
Production U.S.A. .... Modern Talking Pictures, Inc. . . . also
                                       Ford Motor Company
Pure Water and Public Health .... Wisconsin State Board of Health

R

Rabies Control in the Community ..... Communicable Disease Center
Rainbow Harvest .... Modern Talking Pictures, Inc. No. 110

See next pages for movie company addresses.

6

ADDRESSES OF MOVIE COMPANIES AND OTHER RESOURCE MATERIALS

A

ALLIS-CHALMERS MANUFACTURING
COMPANY
Tractor Photographic Department
Tractor Group
Milwaukee 1, Wisconsin

AMERICAN BAKERS ASSOCIATION
Attention: Mr. D. E. McFadden
20 North Wacker Drive
Chicago 6, Illinois

AMERICAN FOOT CARE INSTITUTE,
INCORPORATED,THE
1775 Broadway
New York 19, New York

AMERICAN GAS ASSOCIATION
Film Library
420 Lexington Avenue
New York 17, New York

AMERICAN HEART ASSOCIATION
These films can be obtained from your
local or state heart association.

AMERICAN INSTITUTE OF BAKING
400 East Ontario Street
Chicago 11, Illinois

AMERICAN OSTEOPATHIC ASSOCIATION
Association Order Dept.
212 East Ohio Street
Chicago 11, Illinois

AMERICAN PODIATRY ASSOCIATION
Audio-Visual Council
Dr. Marvin W. Shapiro, D.S.C., Director
1056 Spitzer Building
Toledo, Ohio

AMERICAN RED CROSS
These films can be obtained through
your local Red Cross Chapter

ASSOCIATION FILMS, INCORPORATED
1108 Jackson Street
Dallas, Texas
or:
561 Hillgrove Avenue
La Grange, Illinois

B

BELL SYSTEM TELEPHONE COMPANY
See your local Bell Telephone Com-
pany to obtain movies from the Public
Relations Department of that company.

BETTER VISION INSTITUTE, INCORPORATED
3157 International Building
650 Fifth Avenue
New York 20, New York

BOSTON CONVENTION AND VISTORS BUREAU
125 High Street
Boston 10, Massachusetts

BRYSTOL MYERS COMPANY
Educational Service Department
45 Rockefeller Plaza
New York 20, New York

BUREAU OF COMMUNICATION RESEARCH,
INCORPORATED
267 West 25th Street
New York 1, New York

C

CANADIAN CONSULATE GENERAL
Addresses below serve only the states
listed after each address:

CANADIAN CONSULATE GENERAL
80 Boylston Street
Boston 16, Massachusetts
(Serves: Massachusetts, Rhode Island,
Vermont, New Hampshire, and Maine.)

158

CANADIAN CONSULATE GENERAL
111 North Wabash Avenue
Chicago 2, Illinois
(Serves: Illinois, Indiana, Iowa, Kansas, Kentucky, Minnesota, Missouri, Nebraska, North Dakota, South Dakota, and Wisconsin.)

CANADIAN CONSULATE GENERAL
1139 Penobscot Building
Detroit 26, Michigan
(Serves: Michigan and Ohio.)

CANADIAN CONSULATE GENERAL
510 West Sixth Street
Los Angeles 14, California
(Serves: Arizona, 10 counties in southern California, Clark County in Nevada, and New Mexico.)

CANADIAN CONSULATE GENERAL
215 International Trade Mart
New Orleans, Louisiana
(Serves: Alabama, Arkansas, Florida, Georgia, Louisiana, Mississippi, North Carolina, South Carolina, Oklahoma, Tennessee, and Texas.)

CANADIAN CONSULATE GENERAL
400 Montgomery Street
San Francisco 4, California
(Serves: California—except the ten southern counties.)

CANADIAN CONSULATE GENERAL
1407 Tower Building
Seventh Avenue at Olive Way
Seattle 1, Washington
(Serves: Idaho, Oregon, Washington, Alaska, and Montana.)

CANADIAN EMBASSY
1746 Massachusetts Avenue, Northwest
Washington 6, D. C.
(Serves: Delaware, District of Columbia, Maryland, Virginia, and West Virginia.)

COMMUNICABLE DISEASE CENTER
United States Public Health Service
P.O. Box 185
Chamblee, Georgia

CONTINENTAL ILLINOIS NATIONAL BANK & TRUST COMPANY OF CHICAGO
Education and Training Division
231 South LaSalle Street
Chicago 90, Illinois

CREDIT UNION NATIONAL ASSOCIATION
Public Relations Department
Madison 1, Wisconsin

D

DU PONT DE NEMOURS AND COMPANY, INCORPORATED, E.I.
Motion Picture Section
Advertising Department
Wilmington 98, Delaware

E

EDUCATORS PROGRESS SERVICE
Dept. E.P.S.
Randolph, Wisconsin

EMPLOYERS MUTUALS OF WAUSAU
Film Department
Wausau, Wisconsin

F

FARM CREDIT BANKS
Baltimore, Maryland

Berkeley, California

Columbia, South Carolina

Louisville, Kentucky

New Orleans, Louisiana

Omaha, Nebraska

St. Louis, Missouri

St. Paul, Minnesota

Spokane, Washington

Springfield, Massachusetts

Wichita, Kansas

FARM FILM FOUNDATION
1731 Eye Street, Northwest
Washington 6, D. C.

FLORIDA DEVELOPMENT COMMISSION
Film Library
Carlton Building
Tallahassee, Florida

FORD MOTOR COMPANY
Ford Film Library
Dearborn, Michigan—The American
Road

G

GENERAL MILLS, INCORPORATED
Film Library
9200 Wayzata Boulevard
Minneapolis 26, Minnesota

GENERAL MOTORS CORPORATION
Public Relations Staff, Film Library
General Motors Building
Detroit 2, Michigan

GINN & COMPANY
205 W. Wacker Drive
Chicago 6, Illinois

GOOD NEIGHBOR COMMISSION OF TEXAS
P.O. Box 2116, Capitol Station
Austin 11, Texas

H

HUNTINGTON LABORATORIES,
INCORPORATED
Huntington, Indiana

I

IDEAL PICTURES, INCORPORATED
58 East South Water Street
Chicago, Illinois

Materials may be obtained by writing
the office nearest you:

Atlanta 3, Georgia—52 Auburn Avenue,
Northeast

Baltimore 18, Maryland—102 West 25th
Street

Berkeley 3, California—1840 Alcatraz
Avenue

Buffalo 9, New York—1558 Main Street

Boston 16, Massachusetts—40 Melrose
Street

Chicago 1, Illinois—58 East South Water
Street

Cleveland 14, Ohio—2110 Payne Avenue

Dallas, Texas—1205 Commerce Street

Denver 2, Colorado—714 Eighteenth
Street

Des Moines, Iowa—2204 Ingersoll

Detroit 27, Michigan—15924 Grand River
Avenue

Kansas City 6, Missouri—1402 Locust
Street

Los Angeles 57, California—2408 West
Seventh St.

Louisville 2, Kentucky—616 South Fifth
Street

Memphis 3, Tennessee—18 South Third
Street

Miami 32, Florida—55 Northeast Thir-
teenth Street

Minneapolis 4, Minnesota—3400 Nicollet Avenue

New Orleans 13, Louisiana—1520 Terpsi-
chore

New York 36, New York—233-239 W.
42nd St.

Pittsburgh 22, Pennsylvania—14 Wood
Street

Portland 5, Oregon—1239 Southwest
14th Avenue

Richmond 19, Virginia—219 East Main
Street

St. Louis, Missouri—3743 Gravois Street

INSTITUTE OF VISUAL COMMUNICATION,
INC.
40 East 49th Street
New York 17, New York

J

JAPAN TOURIST ASSOCIATION
45 Rockefeller Plaza
New York 20, New York
or
651 Market Street
San Francisco, California

K

KIEKHAEFER CORPORATION
Film Library
Fond du Lac, Wisconsin

M

McKNIGHT AND McKNIGHT
Publishing Company
Bloomington, Illinois

METROPOLITAN LIFE INSURANCE COMPANY
1 Madison Avenue
New York 10, New York
or
600 Stockton Street
San Francisco 20, California

MISSOURI DIVISION OF RESOURCES AND
DEVELOPMENT
Jefferson Building
Jefferson City, Missouri

MIZRACHI WOMEN'S ORGANIZATION OF
AMERICA
242 Fourth Avenue
New York 3, New York

MODERN TALKING PICTURE SERVICE
3 East Fifty-Fourth Street
New York 22, New York

Films may be booked from the above
address or from the following exchanges.
Book from the one in your area. Each
exchange has an exclusive territory,
and you will be served by one and only
one exchange.

Atlanta 8, Georgia—714 Spring Street,
N.W.

Boston 16, Massachusetts—235 Stuart
Street

Buffalo 2, New York—122 West Chippewa Street

Cedar Rapids, Iowa—701 Third Avenue,
S.E.

Charlotte 6, North Carolina—501 N.
College Street

Chicago 11, Illinois—216 East Superior
Street

Cincinnati 2, Ohio—9 Garfield Place

Cleveland 15, Ohio—1917 Euclid Avenue

Dallas 7, Texas—1308 Slocum Street

Denver 3, Colorado—28 East Ninth
Avenue

Detroit 1, Michigan—4754 Woodward
Avenue

Harrisburg, Pennsylvania—928 North
Third St.

Houston 2, Texas—2813 San Jacinto
Street

Indianapolis 4, Indiana—102 East Vermont St.

Kansas City 11, Missouri—3718 Broadway

Los Angeles 57, California—2400 West
7th St.

Memphis 4, Tennessee—210 South Cleveland St.

Milwaukee 2, Wisconsin—1696 North
Astor Street

Minneapolis 2, Minnesota—1114 Nicollet Ave.

New Orleans 12, Louisiana—815 Poydras
St.

New York 23, New York—21 West 60th
Street

Omaha 2, Nebraska—1410 Howard Street

Philadelphia 7, Pennsylvania—247 South
Broad St.

Pittsburgh 19, Pennsylvania—210 Grant Street

St. Louis 5, Missouri—621 North Skinker Blvd.

San Francisco 5, California—444 Mission Street

Seattle 3, Washington—2100 North 45th Street

Washington 6, D. C.—927 Nineteeth St., N.W.

N

NATIONAL ASSOCIATION OF ENGINE AND BOAT MANUFACTURERS, INCORPORATED
420 Lexington Avenue
New York 17, New York

NATIONAL COTTON COUNCIL OF AMERICA
Audio Visual Section
P.O. Box 9905
Memphis 12, Tennessee

NATIONAL DAIRY COUNCIL
111 N. Canal Street
Chicago 6, Illinois

NATIONAL SOCIETY FOR CRIPPLED CHILDREN AND ADULTS
Audio-Visual Loan Library
2023 West Ogden Avenue
Chicago 12, Illinois

NATIONAL W.C.T.U.
Evanston, Illinois

NEW YORK MUNICIPAL BROADCASTING SYSTEM
Municipal Building
New York 7, New York

P

PRINCETON FILM CENTER, INCORPORATED
Distribution Department
Princeton, New Jersey

R

ROA'S FILMS
(See Modern Talking Pictures, Inc.)

S

SANTA FE FILM BUREAU
Amarillo, Texas—Sante Fe General Office Bldg.

Chicago 4, Illinois—80 East Jackson Boulevard

Galveston, Texas—Santa Fe General Office Bldg.

Los Angeles 14, California—121 East Sixth St.

San Francisco, California—114 Sansome Street

Topeka, Kansas—Santa Fe General Office Bldg.

SCOTT, FORESMAN AND COMPANY
433 East Erie Street
Chicago 11, Illinois

SEEING EYE, INCORPORATED, THE
Office of Public Information
9 Rockefeller Plaza
New York 20, New York

STERLING*MOVIES U. S. A., INCORPORATED
100 West Monroe Street
Chicago 3, Illinois

SWIFT & COMPANY
Ag Research Department
Chicago 9, Illinois

U

UNION PACIFIC RAILROAD
Department of Livestock and Agriculture or Motion Picture Bureau
1416 Dodge Street
Omaha 2, Nebraska

UNITED BROTHERHOOD OF CARPENTERS AND JOINERS OF AMERICA
Carpenters' Building
222 East Michigan Street
Indianapolis, Indiana

UNITED GAS CORPORATION
Public Relations Department
Shreveport, Louisiana

UNITED STATES FOREST SERVICE
Materials are available from the following regional offices:

Albuquerque, New Mexico—510 Second Street
(Serves: Arizona and New Mexico)

Atlanta 23, Georgia—50 Seventh Street, Northeast
(Serves: Alabama, Arkansas, Florida, Georgia, Louisiana, Mississippi, North Carolina, Oklahoma, South Carolina, Tennessee, and Texas)

Missoula, Montana—Federal Building
(Serves: Northern Idaho and Montana)

Milwaukee 3, Wisconsin—710 N. Sixth Street
(Serves: Illinois, Indiana, Iowa, Michigan, Minnesota, Missouri, North Dakota, Ohio, and Wisconsin)

Ogden, Utah—Forest Service Building
(Serves: Utah, Nevada, southern Idaho, and western Wyoming)

Portland, Oregon—729 N.E. Oregon Street
(Serves: Oregon and Washington)

San Francisco, California—630 Sansome Street
(Serves: California)

Upper Darby, Pennsylvania—6816 Market Street
(Serves: Connecticut, Delaware, Kentucky, Maine, Maryland, Massachusetts, New Hampshire, New Jersey, New York, Pennsylvania, Rhode Island, Vermont, Virginia, and West Virginia)

Washington, D. C.—(Serves: District of Columbia)

Users from Colorado, Kansas, Nebraska, South Dakota, and Wyoming should direct requests to Colorado State University, Fort Collins, Colorado

UNITED STATES PUBLIC HEALTH SERVICE
Dept. of Health, Education, and Welfare
Washington 25, D. C.

UNITED WORLD FREE FILM SERVICE
1445 Park Avenue
New York 29, New York

W

WESTERN PACIFIC RAILROAD
Department of Public Relations

Chicago 3, Illinois—105 West Adams Street

Los Angeles 17, California—1709 West Eighth St.

New York 36, New York—500 Fifth Avenue

San Francisco 5, California—526 Mission Street

WHEAT FLOUR INSTITUTE
309 West Jackson Blvd.
Chicago 6, Illinois

WISCONSIN STATE BOARD OF HEALTH
Film Library
State Office Building
Madison 2, Wisconsin

WOOL BUREAU, THE
The Librarian
360 Lexington Avenue
New York 17, New York

7

YOUR EVALUATION OF THIS CURRICULUM

THIS EVALUATION sheet is being attached with the hope that each reader will conscientiously evaluate this curriculum. Please mail this evaluation sheet to the following address at your earliest convenience after you have read the curriculum: Mr. William F. Sniff, Oconomowoc High School, Oconomowoc, Wisconsin.

Your Cooperation regarding this request will be immensely appreciated. Your positive and negative criticisms and suggestions will help the author in preparing future curricula from which you may benefit.

I. Objectives:

A. Does the content of this curriculum satisfy the objectives of a program for mentally handicapped young adults in terms of facilitating personal and emotional adjustment, social adjustment, and economic adjustment as a citizen in the community? Yes. ☐ No. ☐

Comments:

B. Do you feel that this is a practical curriculum for a program at the secondary school level for the educable mentally handicapped? Yes. ☐ No. ☐

Comments:

II. Content:

A. Do you feel that there is content that should be omitted from this curriculum for mentally handicapped young adults? Yes. ☐ No. ☐

Comments:

B. Do you feel that there is content material which has not been included in this curriculum which should be added? Yes. ☐ No. ☐ If so, please comment as to what subject matter you feel should be included:

C. Are there any corrections to which you would call attention? Please list below: